How to Set a Clock at the North Pole:

Volume IX of
The Travels of
Senator & Wendy V

ISBN: 978-0-99150-939-3

Other Titles by Wendy V

Travelogues:
How to Read a Compass in the Dark (2006)

How to Change a Flat on a Unicycle (2007)

How to Start a Fire Under the Sea (2009)

How to Eat a Pizza From a Can (2011)

How to Hitch a Ride With No Thumbs (2013)

How to Draw a Map of the Forest (2015)

How to Book a Flight for Last Year (2017)

How to Take a Drink From a Cactus (2019)

Poetry:
Eventually, Finally (2007)

for Senator—

"...But we are..."

"Adventures are never fun while you're having them."

~C.S. Lewis
The Voyage of the Dawn Treader

Table of Contents

Author's Note

You will, no doubt, recall that my Essential Other still faithfully responds to that initial moniker bestowed upon him: Senator. (I suppose there are those who would refer to him as David or Daver as well.)

Introduction

Depending on the capacity in which people know me, they will describe me as overly cautious or quite adventurous, respectively. Some know me as a planner who truly sees the divine in the details. Others call me spontaneous. I walk by faith while trying not to get my hopes up too high. What then, is the result of this modern embodiment of several blind men touching different parts of the same elephant?

I am exactly the type of person who never discussed marriage with my long-time Essential Other, Senator, though we had been inseparable for the better part of two decades and had even drawn up wills in each others' favor years ago. I am exactly the type of person who had to carefully weigh concerns before accepting his utterly out-of-the-blue proposal. Most of all, I am exactly the type of person who could only be part of such an adventure if it was a completely secret elopement. (Fortunately, Senator is exactly the type of person who can make sense of all of my madness, and therefore, exactly the type of person who loved the idea of a romantic run.) In April 2019, we expressed our deeply committed partnership by exchanging personal vows and joining microphone cables to illustrate the union. All of it took place outside, against the backdrop of mountains and blowing New Hampshire snow. I am still in shock...

We now refer to the week we eloped as "the greatest week of our lives-- *so far*". This book does not contain that story, but it picks up with our travels going forward.

Formalizing our relationship in the Live Free or Die state only gave us the urge to travel more. We have always made our house our home, but our home has never felt so misplaced. We endlessly dream, and then rein it in with practical planning. At any rate, we continue to go.

~Wendy V
September 2019

Chapter 1
So Far:
Late July 2019

Yes, we had eloped. During the first three months of the year, somewhere between working, planning two Civil War weekends in the South, a minor medical annoyance, getting hit by a drunk driver, and a brief three-day stint hunkered down in our home waiting out the polar vortex[*], we worked out the details of our secret elopement. In addition to all of the necessary clothing, accessories, and prop items for our ceremony, we had to bring along extra documents and identification to satisfy the legal requirements. Then there was the fact that we had decided

---

[*] Not sure what a 'polar vortex' is? Fear not, Reader; neither are we. What we do know is that somewhere, way up north, not quite as far as Santa's workshop but considerably farther than Milwaukee, wind currents dash and spin and generally wreak a very cold havoc, pressing wind chills down to almost -60°F, even as far south as Chicagoland. In such cases, people who do not have terribly critical jobs stay home. That means high school teachers who independently publish travelogues and recording engineers who document avant garde jazz have a few days to sleep in, read, and plan elopements. Thank the Good Lord we had plenty of coffee on hand!

to include an intense mountain hike two days before the wedding. I wonder how many people pack their crampons and trek poles alongside their suit and wedding dress?...

Though everything went perfectly, it was still a pleasure to take our first post-elopement vacation to a familiar place that needed almost no planning. It would be our fourth time visiting my parents at their cabin in Ontario. The route and routine were familiar. Only two reservations needed to be made, one of which was at a small hotel we had stayed at previously. No formalwear was involved, unless you count picking out tee shirts that didn't have holes in them. The biggest challenge was planning meals, but even that was easy enough, due to a few years of experience. With my newly updated passport*, we were soon on our way north.

*   *   *

We were off to a good start on that last Thursday in July. The weather cooperated for an easy departure as we eagerly cooperated with one another to get on the road and out of the summer heat and humidity as soon as possible. The first half-hour just felt like my commute to work, but then we turned north. Crossing into Wisconsin later made it feel like vacation. The traffic picked up, but things were moving along, even as we neared Madison, City of

---

*   They day after we returned from running away to the mountains, I immediately applied for a new passport to reflect my legal name change. I was told to allow six weeks for processing. Never the optimist when dealing with the government, I allowed three months. I was so pleased when my new passport arrived in plenty of time. Only for a moment did I fret, when I read my first name with Senator's last name, and for a second thought they had mixed things up. *Oh, right-- that's me now!*

2

Perpetual Construction.[*] I was enjoying the drive, enjoying Senator's company, and really enjoying the fact that he now had glasses that once again made travel a joy instead of a stress.

Not all of God's creatures were quite so happy at that moment. As I cruised along in the left lane, situated in my spot by the steady flow of northbound interstate lanes, I saw a deer. At that instant, I switched mental gears into high alert mode, as all good midwestern drivers do when they see a potentially treacherous Bambi while traveling at high speeds. I must have glanced around, because I remember noting that a car towing a trailer was in the next lane, a bit ahead of me.

As I was filing that information in case it was needed, my brain finished processing the first sight of the deer. In fact, the small doe was not just standing paralyzed on the side of the road, which would have been concerning enough. No, she was taking advantage of the brief gap in traffic to charge straight at us. Occasionally one hears of a drunk person driving the wrong way on the road, but I know of no stories about directionally-challenged deer taking to the highway.

I'm sure my heart skipped a beat (or several), but I did not panic. I managed to swerve into the right lane to avoid the deer, taking into consideration that I did not want to end up as part of the trailer I had seen. There was no time to even warn Senator, but I think he realized what was happening a split second after I did. Thankfully we missed

---

[*] I sincerely believe that if the ground opened up and swallowed Wisconsin, one could still identify the once-capital city by the trails of neon orange cones.

colliding with any other vehicles, but as I was starting to breathe again, and Senator was simultaneously expressing his shock and gratitude for my safe handling of the situation, I realized that I had never looked over before I swerved. In my effort to avoid the trailer, I had instinctively cut hard to the right, without any knowledge of what was there. It then occurred to me that I was effectively pushing Senator into unknown traffic. When the full realization of this hit me, I started bawling. Senator kept asking if I was okay and offering to drive. I think my reaction startled him. In truth I was fine, but it was an unpleasant sensation. I felt like I had haphazardly endangered him. Sometimes driving just sucks.

Eventually I stopped crying, the tension being fully released. I knew I was fine to drive, so I kept at it as I blew my nose and wiped my eyes. We were moving forward, and though we remained on alert for deer or other hazards, the drive was smooth and calm once again. After a while, we left the corn and the interstate behind, trading it in for ribbons of highway that cut through forests. Minnesota loomed.

As we crossed the arrowhead portion of the state, the weather tried to decide what to do. Brilliant sun gave way to intermittent bands of clouds. Rain rotated with harder rain as we lost several radio stations to the crackle of nearby lightning. Senator switched off the radio to concentrate on the road. It was a downright downpour, making the stormy hour and a half feel longer than the previous eight hours.

"It looks like it's finally letting up," I noted. In plenty of time before reaching the tricky-to-navigate border, the rain stopped. We were left with streams of interesting clouds as the sun set somewhere far behind them. I hoped that the storms were out of the way for the rest of our trip. It was more or less what the forecast had predicted anyway.

When it came time to cross the border, we dutifully pulled up to the guard window, stopped the car, and produced two valid United States passports, conveniently held open to their proper pages by our equally valid Illinois driver's licenses. The border guard returned our licenses with a look of irritation. Then the litany of questions ensued, most of which we were prepared for. Despite our informal rehearsals, though, there always seems to be one part of the interrogation that throws us for a loop.[*] This time it was the simple question of where we were staying. We stumbled, confused as to whether he meant for the bulk of our trip, or just for that night. (It turned out to be the first one.)

As we tripped over that one, he demanded (none too clearly) the type of accommodations. "Uh, a cabin, on a lake-- Eagle Lake."

Frankly, I would not have believed us, given our stammer. Still, he probably did not need to interrupt our answer with a curt, "You're not helping me!" In the meantime, he must have run our license plate or scanned our passports to know we were not a threat. He slapped them back into Senator's hand with a sarcastic, "Enjoy your stay." At least we weren't wearing shirts with big American flags on them.

Once allowed to proceed onto Canadian soil, we drove to the same hotel we had stayed at the previous two

---

[*]   I guess that's the point.

years. This particular link in the popular chain always did a thriving business, significantly assisted by the fact that there was not much competition in the area. The vibe was not particularly interesting, but I was amused by the fact that every time we have been there, someone has been taking advantage of the guest grill, which sits right outside the main entrance, at the edge of the parking lot. Senator parked the car temporarily under the canopy so we could go in and register. As we stepped out of the car, a fellow tourist nodded a "hello" in our direction as he flipped whatever he was cooking. Quirky, but friendly.

Inside we learned that our familiar stopover was also undergoing some remodeling. As we walked the hallway to our room, the evidence was overhead. Long lines of exposed cables and pipes snaked above the open ceiling. I wondered what they were fixing or improving. Maybe they were adding electric grills to each room.

We found our room, which appeared neither outdated nor remodeled. Senator and I dropped our gear and went into our systematic routine of checking everything for cleanliness and functionality. "What's your plan for dinner?" asked Senator.

"I don't really have one..."

"Yellow cheese or white cheese?" he quipped, referencing the nearby Subway, whose counter worker had offered us those options for sandwich toppings the previous year.

"Maybe not," I laughed. "There's a new place next door. It's a burger joint, but they might have a veggie or bean patty..."

"That sounds good. It's raining again. Sitting down

to hot food might be nice."

"Yeah, plus it wins points for being thirty seconds away by foot. I'm not feeling too ambitious now."

The place turned out to be louder and more sports-bar-like than we anticipated. They did have veggie burgers and delicious homemade fries though, and at least the televisions were covering the Tour de France, and not some boring ball game. One could not complain about seeing the foothills of the French Alps on the big screen. The food was overpriced, but by paying Canadian cash, it didn't feel like spending real money.[*]

As is typical of us, we unwound from a long day on the road by kicking our feet up on the bed and scouting out a history show. We can't seem to get away from our war studies, and this time it was World War I. We were drawn in by hours of raw unofficial footage, which was sufficiently fascinating by itself. What really set it apart was the fact that it was colorized. Dough boys from a century ago took on new life that brought them closer than ever. Maybe I should consider a career shift to become an archivist. I'm sure there's a big demand for that in the mountains of New Hampshire...

*   *   *

We had an easy start Friday morning. After a light bite at the hotel we made a quick Walmart run for a few bags of frozen fruit, having learned the hard way the first year that it does not survive an 800-mile journey in the cooler. It appeared that the rain had moved elsewhere, and

---

[*] I think it's a combination of the cheerful colours and the strangely slippery texture. Canadian bills are just begging for their own board game!

we were eager to begin the drive into the back country. Jingles and I had a slight scuffle before getting out of town, but she only cost us one block.[*]

I was happy to see that the Canadians were still speeding worse than me. This gave me an edge to make up for the time that we were stopped for construction. If you have to sit in line waiting for a hand-held sign to change from "STOP" to "SLOW", however, you could do worse than overlooking a wilderness of lakes, forests, and meadows. Soon enough we were on our way again.

As we approached Highway 594, the wildlife sightings picked up. First we saw a young adult male black bear nibbling greens on the side of the road, uninterested in us. A little while later we passed a doe with her spotted fawn in the tall grass. This deer, at least, knew her place-- unlike the manic death-defying doe on I-90. Finally an eagle swooped in front of us as we took a shortcut along a farm road. He dropped something he had been carrying. "Maybe he lost his grasp on his lunch," suggested Senator.

"Or maybe he was using God's outhouse," I offered.

By the time we arrived, the drizzle had caught up with us. By the time we finished unloading, it was raining hard. I had hoped to get outside and maybe even canoe, but it was nice to visit with my parents in the quiet, dark afternoon. As I continued to chat with my mom, Senator

---

[*] Jingles, you may recall, is our semi-faithful G.P.S. device. She has now been part of our family for two years, and it has been, admittedly, a rocky relationship. She is definitely most reliable when she is alone with Senator and navigating Chicago streets for him. On vacations, or when I am along, she may or may not cooperate. Senator rightly points out that it's a surprise she works with us at all, given our recent elopement.

took a ride into the tiny town with my dad. "Go ahead and soak up some culture," I joked. After all, the gas station was the biggest gathering spot for at least a half hour in any direction.

When the men-folk returned, I asked Senator if he wanted to walk down to the dock with me. The rain had mainly cleared out, but it was not calm enough to boat. At least we could sit by the water. Senator followed me down the stone steps toward the shoreline. I kept bouncing along, but he stopped. "You just walked by a snake," he announced flatly.

"Ahhhh!" I yelled, appropriately. "Get me some rocks to throw at it!" I checked around by my feet, making sure I was not in immediate proximity of the beast.

"James probably already got all the good rocks," answered Senator indifferently, referring to our young nephew's fondness for rocks.* Given Senator's calmness, I was expecting to see an average garter snake as he pointed to the grass along the side of the steps. I trained my gaze in the direction of his outstretched finger. It was a garter snake, but this guy had obviously been eating well. Either that, or he was an escaped mutant from a science lab. "Geez! That thing must be over three feet long!" I panted.

Senator clapped his hands by the snake, coaxing it back into the brush to haunt some other poor soul. Its long, striped form looked heinously misplaced among the wildflowers. I guess I had been fortunate to have gone that long without ever seeing a snake at Birch Harbour, but it was shocking nonetheless. The behemoth, of course, could not have cared less about me, but I would be on the lookout

_____
* I think he has finally given up trying to eat them.

for him every time I passed that general direction. War had been declared.

We spent some time outside by the water, and then we each found our way to the enclosed porch. A few weeks earlier I had run across a few treasures at a used book sale. I liked the idea of bringing books to leave at the cabin. My parents are appreciative readers, and it is always fun to find an unexpected gem that fits the scene. To my mom I gave a National Geographic photo book on the various regions of Canadian wilderness. I presented my dad with a useful book on how to read the natural signs associated with water. Who knows? It could be useful in he ever takes the boat out for a three-hour tour that goes badly.[*]

Senator was busy digging through an intense narrative of the Polish underground during Nazi occupation. For my part in the impromptu library session, I picked up the first book in a series by Philip Gulley. It centered around a small-town Quaker minister and the holy and wholly ridiculous dramas that humans seem so good at inventing. It was one of the few books that literally had me laughing out loud. I will highly recommend his gentle yet sharply witty style, but a best-selling author hardly needs my endorsement. Perhaps it's an instance of do-unto-others or karma. Maybe someday an author with a virtually nonexistent readership will give me a plug. One can but dream...

I marked my place in my book and set it down next

---

[*] Come to think of it, wasn't it convenient that the guests on the S.S. Minnow happened to have all of those extra clothes and supplies when they were only going out for an afternoon? I mean, a coconut radio can't solve all of one's problems when stranded on an island.

to the digital weather station on the table. Even though it had poured earlier that day, the humidity was comfortable. The temperature was dropping nicely as well. Outside a flute bird was singing happily in approval. I had forgotten there was such a thing as a flute bird. I don't think we have them near our home, although you would think they would be attracted to all of the instruments Senator owns.

I shifted my attention to preparing dinner while still enjoying the backdrop. The four of us settled into our usual spots and broke bread together at the comfortable old dining table set. There was good conversation peppered with family stories featuring members from four generations. We then transported our tales to the porch, where we watched the sky spend the rest of the evening alternating between rain and sun.

At some point, we admitted a lack of any further energy. Someone called it a night, and the rest of us followed suit. Senator stretched out in bed while I opened the window a crack, savoring a cool night in the midst of summer. For the most part, we slept soundly. There was only a brief moment when Senator was struggling with a little congestion. I touched him gently, prompting him to drink some water. Completely oblivious to my suggestion, he only uttered an unconscious, irritated, and humorous response. "What is it that you are trying to do?" The unexpected formality made me laugh. He never did get his water, but the interruption seemed to improve his breathing. When later asked about the incident, he had no recollection whatsoever of talking to me.

*   *   *

Saturday morning we woke up to the news that a

mother duck and her ample brood of ten babies was trailing around near the water's edge. We grabbed some foul-friendly snacks and headed down to the dock. I, naturally, was carefully on the lookout for the serpent that had invaded our Eden the day before. Though I was happy not to see him, I was disappointed that the ducks swam away from us.

"But we're so fun!" I reasoned.

"They might not be aware of that," consoled Senator.

"...And we have food," I pointed out. When I reported the completely irrational behavior to my mom, she explained that they were a more skittish brand of duck than those that usually hung around. They were more prone to caution, and she had not been able to entice them either. *Their loss.*

With the duck matter settled, we sat down to some sustenance of our own. As in the past two years, I concocted smoothies using a blender we had brought from home. I was getting better at the process; I merely made a minimal mess this time. There was only one minor incident where the wild blueberries lived up to their name, escaping in multiple directions while leaving their inky trails behind.

The weather was ideal, so we set out for our first canoe trip of the year. In addition to life jackets and the other necessary safety gear, we had an upgrade. "Here, take this with," my dad instructed. He handed us a waterproof two-way radio for communication with the home base. Now we were really professionals. "Do you know how to use it?" he asked.

"I know Morse code for S.O.S.," I answered proudly, digging back to a fond memory of playing with radios with my childhood friend.[*]

"Well, that's good," said my dad, clearly humoring me.

It was easier to put the canoe in this year. Last year the water level was at a near-record low, necessitating great strategy to dryly embark on a canoe ride. This time the old wooden ramp gave us plenty of length and depth from which to launch. Nevertheless, it did not stop me from submerging myself ankle-deep in the drink. I had slipped on the slimy patch of moss on the ramp.

At any rate, we were off.[†] The stiff breeze was giving us quite a workout, but we had gone out on choppier water. Even so, we were battling the hardest paddle we had ever encountered. Time and time again we changed our directional plan to best work within our limitations. In fact, the wind was so strong that we never switched the side we paddled on. When one of us needed a drink of water, we had to make it quick so the other one didn't completely lose control while working alone. Needless to say, we did not make it to our goal island. Instead, we made an awkward triangle and returned in about half an hour.

"Good thing we had the emergency radio," I joked, as we had never left sight of the cabin.

"Actually, the battery died about five minutes out." *That figured.*

With daily exercise checked off of our list, we sat

---

[*] For the record, no distress calls were needed during their use in the half-block territory in which we employed them.

[†] The windy morning reminded us of a stupid weather report we had recently heard at home. Because it was going to be 82° F and windy on a summer day, the forecast had called it "brisk". This is why I say that at some point northern Illinois became the Deep South.

down to read. I felt kind of bad laughing out loud at the antics in the book I was reading, as Senator continued learning about the life-and-death struggles of 'his people'. Assuming that he did not want to listen to my manic cackling, I changed activities. It was time to start compiling my editing list.

I will shamelessly declare that I am on a God-given mission to declutter the spaces I come into contact with. That Japanese woman on the cable shows has nothing on my organization skills. I am not trying to brag; it's just part of my wiring. While I am by no means a minimalist, I do insist that possessions actually defend their purpose... or at least directly enhance an appropriate theme if merely decorative. I feel this is a fair approach. Senator, to his credit, has not tried to dissuade me in this.

As with any property that has been in the same family for decades, my parents' cabin has acquired many items. Some are meaningful and sentimental. Some are practical and helpful. Some are downright inexcusable. This third category was my target. The year before I had dabbled in my self-assigned project, testing the waters, so-to-speak. As I packed our bags to leave, I took the opportunity to slip two colonial American figurines into a suitcase. I also snatched the old wicker wine bottle carriers inside which the figures were inexplicably nestled, as they spent their last days in the dark recesses of the storage room. No one missed them for at least a week, and their absence probably still would have gone unnoticed were it not for the convenient extra two cubic feet of available space.*

---

* especially when they learned that their combined retail value fell at

During the past year, my mom had also downsized a few unnecessary items, so I took it as a mandate to go forth and do my good work. I had my eyes set on some pretty hefty prizes. "Let me know before you take anything," my mom commanded.

"Don't worry," I assured her, "I have never downsized anything that anyone would ever use. My record is 100% regret-free."

"For who?" I could tell she was not thoroughly convinced. That was okay; we still had a few days to hash out the details. In the meantime, my dad was offering to take us out on the pontoon boat. A ride that did not involve an epic paddling struggle sounded perfect to us.

Soon we were back out on the water. A few dark masses of clouds clumped here and there, but no rain fell. We easily cruised the maze of islands in search of pine forests, boulders, eagles, loons, and anything else that did not look like Chicago. To accompany our journey, my dad tuned in the radio to the only station that came in.

The live broadcast was beamed in from a small city about an hour west. We soon learned from the excited tones of the crowd that it was, indeed, a very special day. As fate and someone with too much time on his hands in far western Ontario would have it, we were listening to a minute-by-minute account leading up to a momentous event. The community had gathered at the harbor with the express common purpose of breaking the *Guinness Book of World Records*' record for the most people wearing plaid. Now before you scoff, Reader, understand that this was serious business. There were strict guidelines requiring

---

roughly $2.46 on eBay

each participant to wear at least two items of verifiable plaid.* There was also an official process for being counted, hosted by an adjudicator to certify the legitimacy of it all.

Now I started to feel guilty. Two days earlier when we had arrived, my parents had amused us with the news of this contest. We had laughed, but I actually halfway entertained the idea of joining the endeavor. Coincidentally, Senator and I each had exactly two items of plaid-patterned clothing with us. (It was practically a sign!) Ah, but then the day's perfect boating weather loomed, and the water's siren song beckoned me away from an hour drive to stand around wearing mismatched clothing and waiting to be counted. Heck, maybe Americans weren't even eligible. Whatever the excuse, I reasoned my way out of assisting in the attempt to break the auspicious record.

"Gee, what if they miss beating their record by four people?" mused my mom. *Exactly what I was thinking!* We were now invested. We listened to two more hours of an odd assortment of American and Canadian tunes from the last forty years and commercials for local businesses so we could glean updates at the breaks. The drama mounted until, FINALLY, somebody important was called to the microphone. After a lengthy explanation of the certification process, he grandly announced that 1,359 plaid-wearers had smashed the previous record of 1,146 such persons, set back in 2015. On cue, Queen's "We Are the Champions" started up in the background, amid the cheers of the victorious. As one interviewee aptly stated, "It's so wonderful to see everyone out here, coming together for

_____

*   patterns need not match

such a great cause!"* ...And they didn't even need us.

Listening to other people break historic world records is a tough act to follow, but my dad navigated us back to the shore to conclude the rest of our day. I wasn't wearing plaid, but I had ambitions of my own. The dinner I was preparing involved tricky timing and popping things in and out of the oven at regular intervals. With Senator's help, it worked out rather well.

"What are these? Did you make them up?" my mom asked.

"There's egg, spinach, peppers, spices, cheddar... I guess you could call them 'egg Zuch-muffins'," I answered, improvising with a bit of my new last name. On second thought, maybe I should have left it 'egg McMuffins®', in honor of all the Scotch plaid.

We spent the remainder of the evening on the porch. As we all chatted, I caught up on some notes. At various breaks in the conversation we each sneaked a chapter or two of our respective books. On the lake we could see some people out in a fishing boat. When darkness fell, they sent up fireworks, putting on a great show. We cheered in appreciation. Maybe they were celebrating the "great cause" that had been won that day. Hopefully they weren't trying to signal for help. If so, we blew that one.

*   *   *

There's always at least one lousy night of sleep on a

---

* The four of us broke into simultaneous laughter when we heard this. Imagine if someone was just tuning in, wondering what "great cause" brought the community together. Welcoming returning veterans? Feeding the homeless? Curing a disease? No-- just a lot of people wearing a lot of plaid. I think Canada's as crazy as we are.

vacation. This trip it was Saturday night. Maybe it was the late-night dessert, or maybe we were too excited about a nearby community making it into the *Guinness Book of World Records*, but sleep did not go well. Due to the lack of sleep, I couldn't make up my mind whether I wanted to go to church or not. I was going to leave it up to Senator, but he threw it back at me. Neither of us was terribly motivated, but we had enjoyed it in the past, so we decided to go. I picked out my best pants*, got ready, and assumed my spot next to Senator in the back seat of my parents' vehicle. We felt like kids.

A few opportunistic mosquitoes had been patiently lying in wait for their bonsai moment. They struck. We swatted. "Ohhh..." Senator and I groaned in unison at the smudge of bug guts on the pristine light gray cloth ceiling. I grabbed a wet wipe from the conveniently placed canister and went to work. We were both surprised and pleased at the effective results. *Stinkin' vermin!*[†]

It was our third time at the small church, and by now we were used to the friendly and casual nature that the congregation exuded. As we waited for the service to start, one man ate a piece of pie in his pew. That seemed like a good idea to me. I noticed a barefoot (by choice) kid in another pew. I was so engrossed in people-watching that I almost forgot the routine of winding around the sanctuary to greet and shake hands with everyone else. As we did so, one older lady slipped a devotional pamphlet into my hand. Just as slyly, her mischievous husband grabbed it

---

[*]   meaning my newest pair from Good Will

[†]   I recently read that, overall, mosquitoes are the most dangerous creatures on Earth. (I assume the article meant aside from terrorists.)

18

back out again, laughing at his lighthearted prank.

We all stood up for the first two hymns. Then the man leading songs invited us to be seated for the third one. As we started the first measure of "I Stand in Amazement", someone felt the need to point out the irony. "How come we always sit for the ones that talk about standing?" It was a fair question, to be sure.

Following the singing was a time to take prayer requests. A few people spoke up. One woman mentioned someone who had broken his or her arm. Though the pastor noted that it was "old news", he included the person in the prayers anyway. (You can't be too careful.)

The rest of the service progressed as expected. There was a brief message, followed by updates on the persecuted faithful around the world. I shifted in the pew, which I was now remembering was too high for my short stature. When your feet don't touch the floor, you get the chance to use all sorts of underappreciated muscles. In proper time the service concluded, and the cheerful visiting started up again. I was glad we had decided to go after all.

In between prayers and listening to people speak in church, I had been trying to decipher the weather. Though it was clear enough for canoeing, the wind would not cooperate. Thinking of the ill-fated attempt in the wind the day before, Senator and I scrapped any paddling plans for the day. I was disappointed, but at least I could walk down to the dock, to the very edge of solid land. My dad was in hip waders, working on removing a couple of big branches from near the boat. I assisted, but mainly watched to make sure his boots did not fill with water and trap him. Thankfully there was no such drama.

When he was done, I went back up to the porch to sit with Senator and continue in my book. I was still enjoying it thoroughly, but I had been depending on the canoe workout. Now I had to think of a substitute exercise. Then inspiration hit.

"Where's Wendy?" my dad asked Senator when he joined him on the porch.

"Marching around the yard," Senator answered casually. I'm told my dad was amused. Senator has lived with me long enough now not to think anything of it. Anyway, I got to check exercise off my list, and at certain points the terrain allowed me to pretend I actually lived around boulders.

Since I had a free afternoon, I decided it was high time to begin the process of streamlining the cabin. A surge of decluttering motivation swept over me. The process I had deemed most reasonable involved a very democratic system, complete with checks and balances. Room by room I went around, making a list of 'potentials' to dump, complete with rationale for each item. The initial list (and accompanying reasons) was then presented to my dad, my mom, and Senator for the first round of voting. Due to his lack of ownership in the property, Senator's vote only counted for half that of each of my parents. Once the constituency had narrowed the list down to one item from each room, the final list would be presented for a second vote. The top three voting-getting items would forevermore be banished from Birch Harbour.

As you can tell, Reader, I put some thought into this endeavor. Mostly my valiant efforts at improvement were met with groans and rolling eyes. Some people just take the right to vote for granted. Meeting my determination, however, they all agreed to play along.[*] In the end, we removed 1.)a leopard print scrap of material, about the size of a small tablecloth, 2.)a random pair of pants that did not fit anyone we could think of, and 3.)dusty fake flowers that had been trying their *darnedest* to keep the 1970s alive and well. I was satisfied. "It's okay, Guys; don't thank me," I humbly announced.[†]

The election was followed by dinner. We ate and watched as the sky tried to decide what to do. Eventually we did have a big storm, complete with dramatically-disappearing islands as the white wall of rain crossed the lake toward us. The porch windows leaked a little bit, but no harm was done. Any further activities would take place indoors, though.

I finished the book I had started the first night. It was a fast and satisfying read, so I could not help but pick up its sequel, which sat right on the end table next to it. It, too, was moving along quickly. I made a mental note not to leave Birch Harbour until I finished it. *Maybe I can drag this out for a month!...*

"Want to watch this with us?" asked my mom. I put down my new book and joined the others for some quality Canadian nature programming. The first show centered around the rehabilitation of orphaned bear cubs. It was a nice concept, but I can't help but wonder why the rescuers felt the need to intervene in nature, especially when the

---

[*] Though Senator made several attempts to merely vote "Present", his newly-garnered legal status in the family ended any discussion of his abdication of duties.

[†] For full list of candidates and respective cases, see Appendix A.

rest of the wilderness orphans manage without them.

The bear orphanage was followed by a show on salmon spawning. Two years earlier we had witnessed salmon swimming upstream in Newfoundland. It was unbelievable how determined they were. Jumping five feet or more out of the water was nothing to them. The scientist in the show confirmed what I had always heard: that salmon go back to their birthplace to spawn. If this is true, though, I figure some must cheat and not go all the way. Otherwise, all of the salmon in the world would be in the same place. Think about it...

*　　　　　*　　　　　*

I almost forgot where I was when I woke up Monday. We had both slept soundly. I was sort of amazed; Senator's sleep patterns are so unpredictable. Maybe it was the excessively elevated ramp of pillows he had created. The dark morning probably assisted us in sleeping in later than usual, too.

It was misting heavily outside. My dad and I rescued a few towels off the clothesline. They had only made it an hour, and I doubt they lost any of their moisture during their brief stint. Now they hung limp over the drying rack in the storage room. Anytime someone showered, we rearranged them all to make room for the newest member of the terry cloth clan.

Overall, the day was built for what I call 'forced relaxation'. We could not canoe or even ride in a motorized boat, due to the weather. It looked like I was going to be able to finish my second book of the vacation. Senator could probably knock out a few more scenes from the Polish underground as well. Even my dad had to take a break from his manly outdoor activities to come and porch-sit with us. Unless you have a health or safety emergency, I don't really think you could have a bad day at the cabin. As they say, "A bad day on the lake is still better than a good day at work!"

Of course, that is provided that you are the type of person who can amuse himself/herself with good company in the middle of nowhere. If you depend on external entertainment (restaurants, bars, clubs, stores, cafés, museums, theatres, grocery stores), you will be sorely disappointed in such a place. The four of us, however, had a grand time just debating the merits or shortcomings of certain Civil War generals as we ate dinner.[*] At one point, James Longstreet's name came up. Although we both have respect for the good general, Senator and I have slightly different opinions on his strategies and effectiveness. "But he was Lee's 'Old War Horse'," I argued. "He would not have valued and trusted him so heavily if he was not excellent."

"He was no Stonewall Jackson," countered Senator. "Besides, he hesitated far too long at Gettysburg."

"He still followed orders..."

"No, he did not fully support Lee, and Lee was not happy. I think he did this elsewhere, too."

Senator was allowing no wiggle-room here. My mom had chosen the diplomatic route, offering only non-

_____

[*] I am still amazed that Senator has plunged in-- head-first-- to his interest in the Civil War. He went from telling me that he did not have much interest in history to reading a 2,800-page narrative on the War Between the States and asking me which battlefield we are going to visit next. "What have you *done* to me?!" he regularly asks.

23

controversial comments here and there. I could see it was time to end this once and for all. I looked over to my father, who retains more historical knowledge than anyone I know. "Tell him Longstreet's *good*... Daddy!" I demanded. The conversation was over. Senator was laughing the hardest. He never saw the daddy card coming. I love a robust family argument, don't you?

After the dinner debate we meandered through a few television shows until we found ourselves watching more history. This show had nothing to do with the Civil War. Instead, it featured a massive estate with a split personality. Any couple who simply cannot agree on the style of their English mansion should have taken notes on it. It was literally split in half, lengthwise. One side was classical, with sleek lines and prim order. The other half (and the one I was partial to) was gothic, with strong ornamentation and drippy, dark tones. While one might suppose that so much square footage dedicated to the art of compromise would make for a happy relationship, such was not the case. At various times, various family members argued, cheated each other, and in more than one instance tried to murder each other. *Nice family!* With that, Senator and I retired to one of only two bedrooms, both decorated in mid-century north woods style, safe in the knowledge that no one else in the house was plotting our demise.

*   *   *

Another night of perfect sleep-- joy! I stepped outside to visit the little house at the edge of the woods. I could see that the lake was calm, but the mosquitoes were vicious. Both can be attributed to the wind speed, which was holding firm at exactly 0.0 miles per hour[*] according to the fancy weatherometer. I was grateful for the good weather, since it was our last day at the lake.

After breakfast we strapped on our life jackets and grabbed the necessary items for a short canoe trip. For an hour and a half we paddled, making our preferred big loop around Sunset and Moose Islands. We got to see a baby eagle in one nest, and we paddled right beneath an adult eagle in another. It was quite a unique view, and the bird was definitely aware of our presence. There were loons and lots of fishermen around, too. Everyone and everything seemed at peace. It was a rare and splendid occasion.

"Ready to head in?" asked Senator.

"Yep, I'm ready." We paddled back and slid our way onto the edge of the shore, and Senator carefully stepped out. I passed the oars and other items to him. He offered his hand as I stepped out to join him, reeling in the rest of the canoe by its rope. Since it was our last day, we portaged the canoe up the hill and gave it a good spray down. I called it 'washing' the canoe, until Senator pointed out the irony of washing the lake effect off with lake water, which flowed through the outdoor faucet. "Good point."

We took a break to read for a while on the porch. I had now passed the point where I was determined to finish my book before leaving. That said, it was easy to put my book down when my dad suggested one more pontoon ride. Again we found our life jackets, sunglasses, and a few other items for our tour.

Out on the lake there were still lots of people

_____

[*] Canadian conversion= 0.0 kilometers per hour

fishing.* The sun was bright, which unfortunately meant that the flies had no problem finding us. One of the great mysteries of lake life is how a boat can leave port with no hitchhikers, yet a dozen or more flies will eventually track it down and board, even if it means they must fly for great lengths. No food is needed to attract them; their sole intent is to harass the passengers-- especially the captain. This, in turn, is a silent declaration of war. Almost as important as the onboard life-saving equipment are the fly swatters that are purposefully stowed in strategic locations. I am slow, but when motivated I can increase my speed. By the end of the ride I had twenty-six confirmed kills. The successful strike campaign was not without casualties on our side, though. We each sustained a few bites, particularly on exposed ankles.

We disembarked and started along the dock back to the shore. I walked with my mom, keeping an eye out for the beastly snake I had seen lurking about the past few days. I wasn't sure she was aware of the intruder, so I broke the news to her gently as we started up the steps. She was brave, but she had no more desire to see it than I did.

Sure enough, though, I spied it in the weeds. It had no fear of us, but it made no motion to approach us, either. With enough aggressive-sounding coaxing on my part, and my mom's walking stick as backup, it slithered off into parts unknown. I made a mental note to check online to see

---

* I suppose "lots" is a relative term. There was still plenty of room to go long distances without getting close to any other boats. It's funny how fast I adapt to less population. Senator is the same way, which means we will probably establish a population limit of somewhere around 300 by the time we choose our next hometown.

if such a thing as canned snake repellent exists. If so, I would probably pay decent money for it...

My woman-vs.-nature battle continued as I made a pit stop at the outhouse. Anytime I open the door, I always do a quick visual scan of the contents. I make sure there is nothing in there with me except the necessary bathroom accessories, the electric bug zappers, and the legendary outhouse-themed decorations.[*] If I see anything living, I kill it (usually with a dramatic mid-air ZAP!) or remove it. Provided I see it first, I can generally manage the situation without calling in the reinforcements.

On this particular trip, I saw a large (not horribly extra large, but still considerably worse than your average annoying house spider) spider. I grabbed the broom and went to kill it, but it escaped and ran from my presence. *Well, I suppose that works, too*, I thought. I then sat down to do my business. The mosquitoes had ramped up, so I kept a racket in my hand to swipe the air in self defense. Sure enough, I zapped two. That was good, but as I focused on the frying of the second one, my gaze caught the spider, who had treacherously reentered the stall and planted itself on the corner of the floor.

"Aaaaahhhhhhhhh!"[†]

I actually did have the presence of mind to try to think of a solution, but I was also hoping Senator was running to my rescue. If I could shove the door open enough for it to stick in place, I could make my escape. On the other hand, that depended on the spider staying put as I went by. Maybe I should just be patient and stay put.

---

[*] Oh, and the country water mill music box

[†] However loud you are imagining my scream, just double it, at least.

Shoot! "Senatooooor!"

My knight arrived, but I suspect he did not sprint. "You okay? Spider?"

"Openthedoorit'sinside!" I spilled out in about a half a second. He was already in the process, carefully trying not to budge the offender onto me. By this time my dad was coming up the hill, too. As soon as there was a sufficient opening, I flew out of the outhouse, my jeans only pulled up as far as absolutely necessary.

I was safe, but the drama was not over. "It ran back in! You gotta' get it!" I informed my dad. I knew the spider was hiding under a little stool. At least it was three against one now.

My dad took the broom and forced the spider out of its hiding spot, bludgeoning it and providing the carcass as proof. "Thank you, you guys!" I finally exhaled, and finished zipping up my pants. "You probably knew it was a spider when I yelled, huh?"

"I thought the snake went in there," admitted my dad.

"I figured spider," said Senator. Then, because he is all things recording engineer, he added, "Your scream was really impressive. I did stop for a second to marvel at the three-point echo you produced on the lake." I'm not sure how I feel about his fascination with the acoustics of the situation. I wonder what my dad's book on interpreting water signs would say about that.

The canoe was dry, so Senator and I carried it up to the garage to tuck it away for the season. The mosquitoes were still vicious, especially in that part of the yard. I guess it's the price you pay for a wet spring that raises the lake level. When we reached the door we quickly ducked inside, careful not to bring along any miniature vampires. It was time to make our last dinner anyway.

The aroma of garlic still drifted in the air as we finished our meal and lingered around the table talking. As always, the time had gone too quickly. "Hey, don't forget to write in my guest book," my mom reminded us. I saw a subtle wince from Senator.

He knew the rule-- every guest had to contribute a little memory to the book-- but he still dreaded coming up with the perfect paragraph. Each year he overthinks it and tries to duck his duty. Then as he's writing, he complains that he's not doing a good job. In the end, he always produces a passage that's appropriate and often touching, but we carry out the ritual just the same.

This time, however, Senator was prepared with an unforeseen bargaining chip. He addressed my mother, "What about a *joint* entry, in honor of our official union this year?" *Oooh, sneaky.* She thought about it for a moment, and then conceded, without even a counteroffer. He was pleased with his victory, but I made sure he did half of the writing.

I curled myself up on the couch to finish my second book. My mom did not own the third book in the series, so I guess I had no excuse to continue reading or refuse to go home. Reluctantly, I got up to go pack a few items. It would make the next day run smoother, and less morning trips to the car meant less moments of mosquito attacks. Among the clothes I tucked the items that had been 'edited' via democratic process.

Senator entered the bedroom. "What are you

doing?" he asked, although he already knew. I grinned. "You better make sure you're not taking anything your mom wants," he warned.

"I'm not. It was all decided with a vote. You were there!" I reminded him. I guess there was just a distinctly strong wave of voter apathy on this particular issue.

Our last night at the cabin concluded with a program about Vancouver Island. The misty, forested haven provided a cool ecosystem for a variety of flora and fauna. There were also a native* tribal community. We watched as the show peeked in on a traditional ceremony, featuring ancestral costumes and dancing. The narrator explained some of the rituals, which I thought had dark and morbid overtones. He also happened to mention that their history included some cannibalism. Do what you like, Reader, but I advise you do not accept a dinner invitation from them.

*   *   *

It was almost as if the mosquitoes knew it was their last chance to feast on the visitors. Senator and I worked quickly to get our last-minute stuff in the car. Despite our best efforts, about a dozen found their way in, and another four or five zipped into the house, plotting against their next victims. My mom was ready, though. "Here, take one," she instructed, as she passed me the second electric racket. Our insect-hunting death squad quickly put an end to any nefarious mosquito plans.

Our packing was finished. We had a few minutes to hang out with my parents, so the four of us parked ourselves in the living room one last time to talk. We had had a great time. Now we had to part and gradually shift

---

*   or First Nations

back to real life, work, and a new school year. "I think someday when we move out of Illinois, we'll just come visit you here. It would be a long commute either way, so no real point in traveling to Illinois," I reasoned.

"Makes sense," my mom agreed.

Eventually we had to hit the road. We said our good-byes and I slid into the driver seat. Senator closed my door and then went around to the passenger side. For the first ten miles we rode with the windows down and the air on full blast. This kept the rogue mosquitoes from landing on us and aided Senator in his shotgun assignment of exterminating them.

We drove along quietly for a while. The traffic was easy and the sky was ideal for driving-- not raining, but cloudy enough to keep the sun from assaulting our eyes. At the border, the guard returned our passports with a disinterested, "Have a day." I looked at Senator, eyebrows raised, and laughed.

I then turned my thoughts toward reflecting on our first trip since our elopement. What a difference a year can make. It had been almost twelve months since Senator had been diagnosed with vertical heterophoria.[*] He was now so calm. He had experienced some dizziness, and he had cracked open the ibuprofen once, but overall there was an amazing difference in his overall comfort level and both of our sleep qualities. We were both so grateful for what might be the best year of our lives (so far).

Right on schedule we pulled into the hosta-lined drive of the bed and breakfast I had reserved. For some reason I had snagged an excellent deal, so I could not resist

---

[*] See *How to Take a Drink From a Cactus*, or just search the condition.

booking it. I almost thought we were in the wrong place. The grand and opulent Tudor-style estate was empty except for the woman who checked us in. As we followed her upstairs, she pointed out a spread of snacks laid out in the main room.

The door to our room opened. Senator and I glanced around. It was elegant and inviting. "Or, I can give you a free upgrade..." We turned around to see our hostess open the door across the hall. "Maybe you'd like this one instead. It's the honeymoon suite."

That was appropriate, so we took her up on her offer, and she led us in. Everything seemed to be on a much larger scale than in a typical home. The tall bed practically required a running start and pole vault. The adjacent bathroom, which easily could have been its own suite, featured a whirlpool that overlooked the back yard gardens. I wasn't sure who would soak in a tub in full view of a large window, but there were curtains. The entire décor scheme revolved around cool colors, glitz, and sparkle. Senator immediately dubbed it the "Fred and Ginger" room. What a gem!*

*   *   *

Breakfast was delivered to our Fred and Ginger room, adding to the feeling of luxury. It reminded us of our new year's eve tradition of watching the magical dance musicals. We sipped our coffee and discussed our own new year. With a teacher in the household, "new year" means August. House projects were looming. There was more downsizing on the horizon. Jobs beckoned. We were already clamoring for fall. All in due time.

---

*   and the room, too

We left the lighter highways behind and entered the interstate for the remainder of the drive home. (That's usually the first nail in the vacation coffin.) In Wisconsin we saw several state troopers posted at several medians and overpasses. Later we learned that someone had gone missing in the Dells region. The national news also informed us that a dangerous prisoner had escaped from Arkansas, and two murderers were still on the loose in Manitoba. We were already missing our tiny, peaceful corner of Ontario. In the early afternoon we crossed into Illinois. Our trip was unofficially over, so we were anxious to get home.

"Everything looks good," I said, as I entered the back door to our house.

"Yes, it does. Welcome home, Brido," said Senator, calling me by my new affectionate and Three Stooges-inspired nickname.

"Welcome to our home (so far)."

Chapter 2
Ain't Never Seen:
Early October 2019

Note: All facts, figures, and quotes in the following chapter are attributed to and verified within the United States National Park Service visitor centers, battlefield sites, and literature at Wilson's Creek and Pea Ridge.

Autumn. We had waited for it, and finally it had arrived. Less than two weeks after we had to run the air conditioning, I was dreading getting out of bed and stepping on a cold floor. Yet, step on it I did. I stumbled into the bathroom squinty-eyed, wondering for the forty-millionth time how it was that I maintained a career that was engineered with only morning people in mind.

As I tried to open my eyes and begin my routine, I at once saw a spider. I recognized that it was a particularly slow species, and it was positioned on a mirror about three feet up from the floor. If one had to encounter a spider on one's rough Monday morning, it was a rather ideal situation for the necessary extermination. I stepped just a few feet out of the bathroom to grab the vacuum from the hall closet. I then plugged it in and handily sucked up the invader, who, as expected, did not put up a fight. Things were going alright, but I let the vacuum run another ten seconds, just to be sure.

I honestly feel badly for Senator on these mornings. I am sure he does not especially relish waking up to the sound of a blaring vacuum cleaner. As I switched off the machine, however, I could hear that he was still asleep. *Great!* I thought, as I started to rewind the cord onto the peg holders.

Then I realized my tragic flaw. Somehow the laziest and perhaps weakest house spider known to man had stayed in the edge of the vacuum hose. I had to give credit to some sort of weird niche it had fortuitously found; there was no way it had been that clever. At any rate, I replugged in and tried to resuck up, but I had lost my subject. I'm fairly certain it was dead, but the idea of it tucked somewhere among the pile of the bath rug did not sit well with me. I began to frantically search.

I was also keenly aware that my carefully patterned morning routine did not build in but an extra few minutes for dealing with unexpected bugs. As my eyes swept up to check the clock, I noticed another spider, (this one black and of a much faster variety) on the other wall. By this time Senator had awoken, but I attribute it more to my frustrated swearing and crying. I was too tired to deal with this, and I was hit with an overwhelming sense of wanting to go home... only I was home. *Where was New Hampshire when I needed it?* At least we would be leaving for a weekend away the following Friday.

Of course, Senator swooped in to the rescue. He killed what needed to be killed and helped me get out the door on time. Later he cleaned the whole bathroom floor. Gifts like that are truly priceless. If I were him, I probably would have been tempted to pull the covers over my head and turn the music up instead.

As it turned out, Senator's day became complicated as well. His recording studio was not fully cooperating, and neither were the eyeglasses that were supposed to make the studio work easier when it did cooperate. Another eye exam might be needed. There were also several interruptions. Some were part of the normal day-to-day events, and others more extraordinary. The one that took the cake was an email from a childhood friend who was going down a very dark path. "Want to take a walk with me after work?" I suggested during my lunchtime call to him. "We can hash out all of our thoughts on the subject..." He took me up on my offer, and early evening saw us hand-in-hand, trying to understand the illogical, and craving the end of the week, when we would be in a much more serene environment.

*   *   *

For about five months we had been planning to take advantage of a three-and-a-half-day-off weekend that I had. Senator kept his dates open, and four days after our crazy Monday we were more than ready to leave town. I had to attend a training for few hours, but it was close to home, so we enacted the plan we had successfully used to escape on other such weekends. In pouring rain and a driving wind, he picked me up and handed me a cup of gas station coffee. I smiled and kissed him before taking a drink. I knew the weak java was not good, but it had the sweet taste of freedom as we made our way to the interstate.

The forecast had called for rain during the entire drive, but a few hours into our rolling conversations, the clouds broke in the southwest. In fact, the last two and a half hours were punctuated by a piercing blaze that cut through the windshield unrelentingly. We continued to discuss everything from politics to classic monster movies, all the while anxious for the events of the weekend. Saturday and Sunday daytime hours would be devoted to more Civil War battlefield exploration. The evenings would then switch gears to family time hanging out with my sister, her husband, and their kids.

Missouri is always a strange place in which to drive. Some patterns have improved over the years,* but one dastardly practice still exists. Missouri drivers do not believe in changing lanes to allow oncoming cars to smoothly merge onto the interstate. Or if some drivers do, they are clearly not traveling on I-44. Aware of this tenet of Show-Me State religion, we played the game, but to no great pleasure. *"They* must have really had fun entering the highway," I said sarcastically, pointing to a sight we had never witnessed. Two double school buses caravanned down the road. The black spray paint that covered their original district or company names added to the feel that they were run-away circus wagons from some time-defying era. It raised multiple questions, none of which we were able to answer.

Before too long we left the arch and St. Louis behind

---

* (no doubt due to my criticism of Missouri drivers in earlier books in this series)

us. Traffic settled down somewhat as dusk fell, and we completed our day's drive. We were close to the reserved room's location. "What does Jingles say?" asked Senator.

"We're on the right road. It should be easy to spot; it's a large manor with open property around it." True to the photos, we pulled up in front of a white-columned estate. Despite the bright and almost-full moon, I could see a beaming chandelier through the glass of the foyer. There was no doorbell, and no one answered our knock, so we let ourselves in.[*]

The stairway wrapped itself up both sides of the entryway to the second floor. From one side we could hear several voices. They seemed to be chatting and laughing and generally enjoying themselves. Perhaps we had interrupted the family's dinner. We tried the make-subtle-noises-and-hope-someone-notices-us technique, which, of course yielded no result. *But it always works in the movies*, I thought. "Well, I guess we should call somebody," said Senator. It was the only reasonable alternative, so I dug the phone number out of my purse while he turned on his phone.

After a few rings Senator began explaining our situation. In another moment a man emerged from behind a door I had not noticed, ending his conversation with Senator, whom he could now see. "Hello! Welcome!" said the friendly face. The man introduced himself and explained that our room had been changed. Originally I had booked a modest room, but we were about to be upgraded to the "in-law apartment". As he walked us

---

[*] As I write this I realize that we have done this several times throughout our travels. One days it's bound to backfire...

down the basement stairs, the natural question on our minds was whether said suite included someone's in-laws.

Happily, it did not. Despite its palatial size for a downstairs apartment, we were alone. In addition to the ample bathroom, living room, and dining area, we had a huge bedroom. We also had access to a full kitchen (which we did not use) and an exercise room (which we definitely did not use). Redesigned, it easily could have been a three-bedroom apartment. "This is the second time a reservation upgraded us in less than three months!" I marveled, although I still wondered if we were taking someone else's place.

We dropped our gear, double-checked the lock on the door that led to the rest of the house, and let ourselves out the private entrance. I shivered slightly, relishing the crisp autumn night we had both been anticipating. "I'm good with just grabbing a sandwich and bringing it back here," I mentioned.

"That sounds perfect," answered Senator. "It would be a waste not to take advantage of such a huge suite." An hour later we were settled in, cleaned up, and finishing overstuffed vegetable sandwiches. Once we figured out the newfangled television service, we even found an old movie starring one of our favorite character actors from the 1940s. "This vacation's starting out pretty great," declared Senator.

"I agree. Want a granola bar?" I offered. "They're not too healthy-- still fun," I joked.

We watched another hour or so of t.v. and found ourselves getting sleepy earlier than expected. "I think I could go to bed soon," yawned Senator.

It was contagious. "Me too," I copied. For some

reason I felt I had to justify our lack of energy. "We were both up early, and it was a long day. Let's get some sleep now, and we'll be ready for the real fun tomorrow."

It was no surprise that we both drifted off shortly thereafter. What was a surprise was the BANG! that broke the deep silence in the middle of the night. I was jarred out of a sound sleep, thinking something had fallen outside. "No, it's inside," said Senator as he fumbled for the lamp switch. Now I sat upright, quickly confirming that our handguns were within reach.

"*That's* what it was," announced Senator calmly. I looked by his side of the bed. A stupid panel from a plumbing access hole in the wall had fallen down. The magnets that held it to the hole's frame were not quite strong enough. We both wondered how it had stayed up so long, and why the person who had hung it had not simply used hinges. Whatever. It was staying off for the rest of the night.

"Good-night again," I whispered. Senator snuggled back down and we resumed the business of heavy snoozing.

*   *   *

The alarm sounded its frantic series of four beeps. Senator smacked down the top bar, ending its high-pitched demands. We lay there a moment or two before remembering that we had a full day planned. As he stepped out of bed and grabbed a few items from the suitcase, I ran to the window to look outside. The sun was up, but a beautiful layer of sparkling frost covered our vehicle. Like a nut I went to the door to open it, just for a moment, to feel the October chill. Senator joined me, and we stood there quietly for a few seconds. Our week was definitely on an upward trajectory.

As we got ready, we tried to remember the directions regarding breakfast. Our host mentioned that we could come upstairs or he could bring breakfast down. As his wife was out of town and he was managing the place by himself, we told him we were flexible. We were fine with grabbing a plate to bring downstairs, but once we finished the phone call neither of us could remember where the conversation had ended. What had been decided?

Just as we were about to leave the in-law apartment and venture upstairs to investigate, Senator noticed a text message on his phone. Our host had used our number (garnered from our initial call to him when we arrived the previous night) to send a text to ask if we were ready for coffee. In case you are new to this series, Reader, I will tell you upfront that we are not technology-savvy in any way, save what is absolutely necessary for our jobs. As such, neither of us had ever sent a text message, and neither of us had any desire to do so. Frankly, I find them annoying, but here we were, presented with an easy way out of the awkwardness of not remembering the breakfast procedure. "Here goes..." said Senator, as he gingerly worked through the buttons to respond in the affirmative.

The response was instantaneous. I think our host may have asked another question, but by the time we got around to answering that, he was already gently tapping on our door. We greeted our happy coffee elf, and he unloaded water, two mugs, and a pot of a very strong blend, hand-selected by his European wife. We then took him up on his offer to bring down breakfast.

It was hard not to smile as we anticipated our day at Wilson's Creek and our evening with family. (The baked French toast with fresh berries and real maple syrup helped, too.) "You know," I said, between forkfuls, "tonight is the big event with the nephews."

"Oh, I know!" answered Senator. We were fully aware of our commitment to a cozy hour watching *It's the Great Pumpkin, Charlie Brown!* with a three-year old and a five-year old. Though Senator and I watch it together every Halloween, it had been many, many years since either of us had watched a Charlie Brown movie with a kid. Rumors of hot chocolate and soft blankets had been circulated as well.

We finished our decadent morning feast and hit the road heading west. As we drove we observed the soaring wildlife overhead in the bright sunlight. An eagle was riding the breeze, as were several vultures. The turkey vulture population had been noticeably increasing in several parts of the United States during the past few years. I don't know if that is a good sign or a bad sign. Possibly it is just another natural cycle.

As Senator guided us toward our first battlefield, I reviewed the situation surrounding the battle. In April 1861 the country officially went to war-- with itself. The population understood that it was serious, but they had no concept of how long or devastating the conflict would be. Boys on both sides were afraid they wouldn't get to see action before it was all over, which most estimated to be in a few months. The first major battle, in Manassas, Virginia, quickly dispelled notions of the war as a glorious lark.

In the West, years of proslavery/antislavery tension within both Kansas and Missouri left the region ripe for an explosion. Neither state had seceded, but the matter of loyalty to the Union was far from settled. When President Lincoln called for four regiments from Missouri, Governor Claiborne Jackson, a Southern sympathizer like many Missourians, flatly refused. In fact, he moved to seize a federal arsenal at St. Louis. Jackson and his shadow government were countered by U.S. General Nathaniel Lyon, who positioned men near Springfield, close to the Confederate troops of General Sterling Price, General Ben McCulloch, and General Nicholas Bart Pearce.

Ironically, both sides were planning surprise attacks. Lyon's men got the edge, eventually holding a position on the later named "Bloody Hill", near Wilson's Creek. The Pulaski Arkansas Battery responded with three relentless assaults, gaining ground but failing to take the hill. On the other hand, Union Colonel Franz Sigel lost an engagement at Sharp's farm, and the steadfast Lyon was mortally wounded leading another charge. The Union defeat had taken place just weeks after the rout at Manassas, further solidifying the desperate need to hold the strategic state of Missouri.

We entered the visitor center and talked with the rangers at the desk. They supplied us with a map and told us about the little attached museum. They also invited us to view the documentary film, provided someone could round up a replacement light bulb for the one that had just burned out in the projector. Apparently even national battlefields have to change light bulbs at inconvenient times.

Senator and I followed the loop through the displays

related to the Wilson's Creek (or Oak Hills) Battle.[*] The first one focused on slavery, which, though not the underlying cause of the war, cannot be discounted as the best illustration of a hotly contentious issue. We then circled around to learn more about the terrifying guerrilla warfare that swept through the Kansas-Missouri border area for years. During the violence, distinctions were not always made between specific targets and innocent bystanders. Though President Lincoln sent peacekeeping reinforcements, many counties joined rebel forces to set up the Missouri State Guard. With its own civil war raging inside its borders, it is no wonder that Missouri saw the third greatest number of battles, after only Virginia and Tennessee.

"What do you have there?" I asked. I poked my head around to see what was in Senator's hand. My brief pit stop in the bathroom had been enough time for him to acquire another book for our ever-mounting history library. I think he expected me to ask why he was buying it. Instead, I grabbed another one off the shelf and added it to the pile. For two people who generally hate shopping, we can do a lot of pocketbook damage in a visitor center gift shop.

I slid into the seat and clicked on my seatbelt. Senator did the same. Our first stop on the driving tour

---

[*]   Usually I am aware of both names for battles that were named differently by the North and the South. For some reason, Oak Hills had escaped my radar. Given the numerous oak groves throughout the area, I wondered why the creek got top billing over the trees. In fact, I have often wondered why one name seems to stick over the other in so many battles. There does not seem to be a correlation to the winner, so maybe it comes down to whatever the early papers were calling it.

took us to a trailhead that bordered Gibson's oat field and meandered down along Wilson's Creek. It was a beautiful, quiet setting-- perfect for a midday walk to transition our minds to the actual land. We picked up our pace, working up a mild sweat. Many more stops awaited us.

Next we drove to the Ray house. This mid-sized farmhouse served as a field hospital and the recovery location for General Lyon's body. Across the small apple orchard its spring house provided water as needed. Sources state that as the battle raged, Mr. Ray looked on. His wife, their nine children, a slave woman, and her four children all hid out in the cellar. The home was closed, but we peered into the windows, trying to imagine the chaos the structure once witnessed.

We drove a little further, stopping at overlooks near other parts of Wilson's Creek and Sharp's cornfield. In the background were woods where Confederates fled for cover from Sigel's attack. It occurred to me that I had greatly underestimated the significance of this battle. I would not be making that mistake as we approached the Bloody Hill.

"How are we doing on time?" asked Senator.

"Pretty good, but it looks like there's a trail with a few stops, so we should probably step it up if we want to stop back at the visitor center." We grabbed some water and the camera and hoofed it up the rolling trail to the hilltop. The sun's intensity increased, but a stiff breeze helped. Soon we passed the sites of a few battery units. Continuing into the forested part we came across General Lyon's marker. He fought fervently, famously declaring that he "would rather see... every man, woman, and child in the state dead and buried" than give Missouri the right to override the federal government's sovereignty. The path then led deeper into the woods, passing a mass Union grave, before leading to a clearing that overlooked the Edwards cabin.

"Wow, it's really warm! How are you doing?" I asked Senator.

"I'm alright."

"Watch your step there," I said, indicating a washed out trough in the center of the trail. "I've got water here, too, if you want it. I'm thirsty, but my bladder's on 'full'."

We reached the visitor center in enough time to complete the necessary action that would once again allow us to consume more water. As I again came out of the restroom, Senator was again gazing at the books. This time he was not buying. "Hey, they got their light bulb," he informed me.

The ranger at the desk overheard us. "Yes, I am going to start the film in just a few minutes if you would like to watch it." Perfect timing-- absolutely we wanted to see it. We filed into the theatre and selected our seats. As always with national park films, the narration tied together the events we had read about as the historical drama unfolded in full action. Half an hour later we were discussing more thoughts on the topic and our gratitude for having so many important places preserved, protected, and made accessible to the public.

We were right on schedule, which meant sufficient time to get cleaned up before going to my sister Heidi's house. It only took fifteen or twenty minutes to reach our hotel, and Jingles and I were in harmony, which always helps. Senator parked and I walked in to register. A moment later he joined me. The desk attendant was processing the check-in paperwork, but I was reading the note next to a toy train that had caught my eye. The cute decoration was a way to gently break it to guests that a loud train regularly rumbled by. "I guess we did just drive under a train bridge before turning in here," I reasoned. We both liked trains; I supposed we would find out exactly how much.

"I'm really sleepy," said Senator.

"Me too. I guess it was the walking and the fresh air. Need a rest before we go?"

"No way! We've been looking forward to this for weeks!" I was glad he was ready to go. I called Heidi and told her we were on the way.

It was only another fifteen minutes' drive to Heidi's house, and it all went smoothly until we were literally one block away. Somehow we went the wrong way and wandered around a few times before turning the right way. In fairness, I have to share the blame with Jingles on this one.

As expected, the kids were wildly excited when we arrived. I remember the thrill of having company when I was a child. Now I was one of the honored guests, drawn into playing 'dumpster' almost before I could finish saying my hellos. In case you are ever so fortunate, the rules are fairly simple:

1.) Find a large empty cardboard box, preferably from a small appliance.

2.) Cram any and all available objects up to and including toys, pillows, stuffed animals, younger siblings, etc. into said box.

3.) Proceed with great squeals of delight as box flaps are smashed down to duplicate satisfying crushing mechanism.

4.) Occasionally check to make sure all living parties are accounted for.

There you have it: hours of fun for the whole family!

My sister lives seven hours away, so a trip there meant a bit of pre-planning. Two or three times I emailed her asking if she would be interested in a few items we were downsizing. In each case she said she might have a use for the item, so we added it to the pack pile. "What else can we give her?" asked Senator, halfway joking.

He was right, though. The way to do it was to walk around the house and see if anything else would benefit her family more than ours. That was how we came to transport several boxes and bags to Missouri, one of which contained old bits of Halloween costumes, including a top hat. It is interesting how children almost invariably see the unintended purpose of an object. "A magic hat!!!!" proclaimed the five-year old. His younger brother was not far behind. Even their one-year old sister toddled in a little closer to the magnificence.

The next hour was filled with a stream of miraculous appearings of all manner of objects (mostly recycled from the cardboard box 'dumpster'). That hat was amazing. Even more amazing, though, was my sister's perfected take on Chicago-style pizza. In southwest Missouri, that is a great feat indeed!*

---

* There's an old saying that pizza is like sex: even when it's bad, it's still pretty good. While the first half of that adage may be true, I can

After dinner it was time for the main event. The five-year old carefully stowed the magic hat and claimed his spot in full view of the television. The three-year old crawled into my lap, snuggled comfortably next to Senator. Heidi supplied the boys with their promised hot chocolates. Our brother-in-law Philip, baby in one arm, started the dvd. We were all set for the grand viewing of *It's the Great Pumpkin, Charlie Brown!*

Disappoint it did not. Six-and-a-half serious Charlie Brown fans[*] thoroughly enjoyed the classic Halloween cartoon. Though I believe I have seen this movie almost every year of my life, my sister brought keen new revelation to Linus' ill-fated vigil. "Wow, he searched everywhere for the most sincere pumpkin patch. Pretty fortunate that it was only a few steps from his house!"

As if the main feature wasn't enough, there was also a bonus movie on the dvd. As divine intervention into our wonderful weekend would have it, *It's Magic, Charlie Brown* made it a double feature. Out came the top hat, now an interactive prop. Though the kids had not mastered turning us invisible by the time they had to go to bed, there are still hopes on their part.

After multiple rounds of "good-nights", and one parent-instituted punitively subtracted piece of candy from the bags we had brought the nephews, they cooperated and went to bed. Now it was time to do what visiting aunts and

_____

definitely account for bad pizza. Ironically, the worst pizza I ever had was in St. Louis. It was so dull and skimpy that I could have easily polished off three larges by myself. It was more of a glorified cracker really. On second thought, I've had much better crackers.

[*] The baby was a little distracted, but she's showing signs of interest.

uncles do when the nieces and nephews retire for the evening. Yep, we listened to funny stories about them from their parents. The conversation was enhanced by warm apple crisp my sister had made as well, but I was laughing so hard that it almost hurt to eat.

One of my favorite tales was when Philip went to pick up their five-year old son. Another little classmate wanted to know if he was his son's "new daddy". I can only imagine what that kid is telling people. After all, last year at our house he insisted that his brother wasn't really in their family. "We're just giving him a ride," he explained without cracking a smile.

It was time to head back to the hotel for the night. It had been a supremely satisfying day. The balance of a serious trek around a Civil War battlefield and a lounge on a couch with a happy and energetic household was unique, but somehow it worked. "And you know what we *didn't* see today?" I asked Senator, bringing him into my thoughts midway.

"What's that?" he bit.

"At no time did we see kids holding electronic devices and staring at screens like zombies."

"You're right; that's good." It was good, and normal, and refreshing in a world that is rarely any of those. "Yep... because we know so much about parenting!" added Senator jokingly. We both laughed as we stepped into our hotel room.

Senator and I curled up under the covers, glad for a cool night. We talked for a few more minutes and then heard the fast, massive rumble of the train. It was actually kind of pleasant. It never did wake us up, but I heard it again when I happened to wake up for a brief time during the night.

*   *   *

Sunday morning we rose and got ready for part two of our weekend. Over a hot breakfast in the hotel we discussed our plans to drive down to Arkansas to Pea Ridge Battlefield. "I'm ready," I announced.

"What does that mean? You have extra ammo?" Senator was referring to the months I had spent in occasional and mild trepidation of the snakes. While I am aware that snakes exist, and that as a person who enjoys hiking and traipsing around battlefields I could potentially encounter them, it was the Department of the Interior's own literature that made me apprehensive.

Instead of a generic notice about general common-sense safety around plants and animals, the website for Pea Ridge specifically warned of four varieties of poisonous snakes. *Four!* This information was repeated in a brochure I read. As a result, I had determined that I/we would only walk away from the car far enough to read the plaques that accompanied the driving tour. No snakes were going to be clamping onto Wendy V! I assume Senator thought I was overreacting a bit, but we would not miss out on anything. We would still be able to hit all of the key spots.

It was not as cool as it had been Saturday, but it was another comfortable autumn morning as we drove south to Arkansas. I had not realized there were so many cattle ranches in southwest Missouri. We saw all manner of cows, cowlets,* and even a few long-horn steers, which we had never seen before. It made it feel like we had gone even

---

* Yeah, yeah, I know.

further from home than we actually had.

Through the countryside we rolled, eventually crossing into Arkansas. I thought it would look similar to Missouri, but both Senator and I noticed an instant difference. The forests were closer to the road, and the vegetation grew thicker. Overall it just felt wilder, darker, and more rugged. Something about the drive to the battlefield was enshrouded in mystery. Maybe it was just the region, which appeared to be populated with folks who were more independent and less interested in polished civilization. I liked certain aspects of it.

Senator drove into the parking lot and found a snake-free spot. Admittedly, I glanced at the ground for a second before exiting the car. Actually, there were no serpents to be seen anywhere on the visible premises, so I proceeded in cautious optimism. Inside the also-snake-free visitor center, we were greeted by a ranger.

"Hello, folks. Where ya' from?"

We answered his question, and then I threw one of my own to him. "Okay, what's the deal with the snakes here? Because we've been all over the South visiting battlefields, and you guys are the only ones to point out the danger of poisonous snakes. Is this for real, or just a legal thing?"* Thankfully we were assured that as long as we stayed on main trails, we would not encounter any deadly critters. The guy seemed trustworthy. Plus, I figured the

---

* In retrospect, I'm sure we did not need to tell the man that we were from the Chicago area. He certainly could have gleaned the knowledge from my use of such phrases as "what's the deal", "you guys", and "legal thing". While asking such imperative questions, I'm guessing my far south suburbs accent came out as well.

53

cool temperature was on our side. He did, however, ask if we knew about chiggers. I had heard of the bugs, but I had never heard of anyone dying a twisted, painful death because of them, and, unlike a poisonous snake, they were not scary enough to have been featured in a Sherlock Holmes mystery. I felt good about the situation.

The first item I saw in the visitor center was an ambulance. It was a rough wooden wagon, and not one I would want to be transported in while injured. Still, it was the most comfortable ride of their day. Once the shocks were enhanced, officers took notice; apparently several of them treated themselves to riding in ambulances when they needed to travel. I can only hope and assume they gave up their luxury wheels when they were needed for their real purpose.

Senator called over to me. "Looks like the film's about to start. Want to go in?"

"Yes, let's do that," I answered. Our eyes adjusted to the dark as we found our seats. I took Senator's hand and we settled in to gain some background about the Battle of Pea Ridge. From what we had learned the day before, it seemed like the next logical event on the Missouri-Arkansas border.

About four months after Wilson's Creek, General Samuel Curtis was placed in command in southwestern Missouri, with the objective of repulsing Confederates and Confederate-sympathizing Missourians out of the state. Within two months, Curtis has pushed General Sterling Price back south into Arkansas. Far from defeated, Price joined forces with General Benjamin McCulloch's and General Earl Van Dorn's men, with Van Dorn at the helm, near Pea Ridge. His plan was to swing around and attack the Union troops from the north. To the detriment of many, he did not account for how hungry and exhausted the men were. His master plan of sending McCulloch and cavalry leader General James McIntosh around the west side before rejoining was ill-conceived. Both generals were killed in intensive fighting, and their men were scattered, unsure of their next orders.

Initially Van Dorn's east side assault was going considerably better than the western half. By nightfall, he held the Elkhorn Tavern. The next morning, however, it was another story. Curtis counterattacked, turning the tide. Critically low on ammunition, Van Dorn retreated, further assuring Missouri's position in the Union.

We took a few minutes after the documentary to look over the paintings that lined each side of the theatre. I think there were seven or eight, perhaps by the same artist; I'm not sure. Each invited the viewer into a deep moment that reflected the anticipation, exhaustion, or uncertainty of life on a battlefield of complicated loyalties. They complimented the other displays in the museum nicely. We could have spent longer getting lost in the paintings, but it was time to go outside.

A strong autumn breeze swept across the open field adjacent to the parking lot. Senator opened my door, offering me the passenger side. "Are you sure you feel like driving?" I asked.

"Yeah, I'm doing great," he responded.

"Okay, just let me know..." I took a swig of water and passed the bottle to him. "We start the driving tour over there," I indicated. It began along the southern

55

boundary of the battlefield, from where the Union *assumed* the Confederacy would engage. The Trail of Tears also criss-crossed the land. There was not much to see there, but we stepped out a few times to read posted information. Each time I briefly glanced around to make sure no serpents were ready for battle, either.

We rounded the corner and crept up on the site of the Leetown Battlefield. It was still being used as farm fields. Rolled bales of hay dotted the large open space, and the wind fired up a bit stronger. Though Confederate forces attacked from the nearby woods, they were not successful. Worse, they lost the top two commanders whom Van Dorn had sent to lead the western coalition. General McCulloch and General McIntosh were dead, and the hungry, spent troops were in disarray, unsure of orders.

The next stop was unusual and unique to only the Pea Ridge Battlefield. Though native Americans had participated in other military conflicts both before and during the Civil War, a section of the western part of the battlefield saw the greatest concentration of natives fighting during the war. Around 1,000 Cherokees fought on the Confederate side. Eventually they were driven back to the forest, but other Cherokee regiments remained ready in reserve.

We continued to an overlook on the west side. A stone barrier guarded us from the drop-off to the dense trees below. The breeze strengthened as it blew at us from the valley below. The place reminded us a lot of Shenandoah National Park, except there were many more oaks. Most importantly, there were no snakes here, either.

The driving tour then led us across the northern

stretch to the eastern half of the park. There another overlook promised a vast view. I was a little hesitant because it required a ¼-mile walk, but Senator easily talked me into going. It helped that it was on a wide, paved sidewalk. A thin or overgrown trail would have had me hiding back at the car.

"This is great!" declared Senator. He was right. It was one of the best views of any battlefield we had ever visited. Not only did the overlook provide a wide vista over the rocky ledge, it offered a rare look onto an entire battlefield at once. Had someone been standing in the same spot on that fateful day in March 1862, he would have witnessed about 10,000 troops poised to engage on the field below. Unfortunately, the rocks immediately before us played the same role as those at Stones River. First they were welcome shelter. Then they were a hindrance that trapped troops. The scene was sobering.

Feeling confident in my snakeless day, I was eager to continue on to Elkhorn Tavern and learn its complex history. This reconstructed building illustrated the original one that served as a stop on the Telegraph Road. Early in the conflict it became Union headquarters, but later Van Dorn claimed it for Confederate headquarters. Wounded men from both sides were treated there. Ultimately, it rested in U.S. hands... until Confederate guerrillas burned it down a year later. Ultimately undaunted, the family quickly rebuilt it and stayed for many generations.[*]

_____

[*] I wonder how many homesteads remain in families for more than a generation or two these days. I imagine it's not many. Though my great-grandparents' home was only inhabited by one subsequent generation, their daughter stayed there into her eighties, keeping the

Our last stop at Pea Ridge Battlefield took us down to the field we had seen from the overlook. Cannon stretched a great distance, spaced to represent the two armies as they faced off. It is still hard for me to believe that men fought this way. It was so obviously brutal. Why fight in the open? Then again, thinking back to our visit to the Wilderness Battlefield in Virginia, I must admit the woods were often no better.

"Let me know when it's flashing," directed Senator. He was adjusting the tripod to take a photo of us before we left Pea Ridge. "Is it going?"

"Now!" He trotted over to my side, estimating where he would be in the shot. The camera timer expired, and we heard the familiar click. Just then, something caught the corner of my eye.

"Hey, look," I pointed. Near the end of one of the artillery lines was a doe. She was standing in the sun, looking peaceful in the autumn afternoon rays. Frankly, she did not care whether Missouri stayed in the Union or not.

I slid into the passenger side while Senator went around the car. Though he started to drive, the motion, the music, and the musings of all we had seen soon rendered him sleepy. He pulled over, and we switched. Soon he was out, contentedly dozing. I was mildly tired too, but I was too excited about our evening. Like the day before, we would make a quick stop to clean up and then head to my sister's home.

When we reached the hotel, I called Heidi. "Hey, we're a little ahead of schedule. Is it okay if we come early?"

---

home in the family for about a century.

"Of course! See you soon!"

If possible, our nephews were even more excited than the night before. Happy shrieking ensued and general mayhem greeted us. Ready or not, we were in. By now "Daver" was an assumed full-fledged member of their fun.[*] All manner of repurposing was taking place, using everything from trucks to teacups in the construction process.

Likewise, the magic hat was still a crowd favorite. Item after item was magically produced from it in grand succession. Senator then introduced the fine art of distraction, showing the boys how to cleverly divert the audience's attention. "Look! A pigeon!" he exclaimed, pointing to a random spot on the wall. Intrigued by the use of deception, the five-year old upped the ante. Conscious that not every audience member might be as gullible, he adapted the skill. "Look! There's a monster outside!" His Uncle Daver fell for it, in great exaggeration. Oh, the manipulative power!

My sister interrupted the masterful legerdemain to call us to the kitchen for dinner. Her homemade bread smelled wonderful, as did the cozy crockpot of broccoli-cheese soup. We couldn't wait to dig in. For the under-six crowd, however, she had to use a little illusion of her own. Some parents of young children have raised the talent of

_____

* As you no doubt know, Reader, Senator has several names to which he answers. As we acquired nieces and nephews, we figured 'Daver' would be an easy and unique one for them to learn. There was a temporary variation of "Mr. Daver" by the five-year old, which we attribute to his school experience, where it seems all those adult-types demand some sort of title. I think his younger brother may have corrected him. If so, it probably did not end well.

disguising and bargaining vegetables to a whole new level. I tip my magic hat to them.

"K'I have mo bwead pwease?" asked the three-year old, politely.

"Eat more soup," instructed my sister.

"I awweady did eat sommmmme," he countered.

"Another spoonful."

"Awwight. One mo, and dats aw I can do." With furrowed brow he gulped another stoic spoonful. The negotiations were proceeding well. "Okay, dats it," he announced. "K'I have mo bwead pwease?"[*]

The three-year old was still not as picky as the five-year old. For about two years he would not eat meat. The problem was that he also did not care for most vegetables. Gradually his accidental stint as a reluctant vegetarian ended, but he was still suspicious of the origins of his meal. When his parents explained that meat came from animals, he knew they were grossly misinformed. As he reasoned, "I ain't never seen a meat walkin' down the street!" His rhythmic logic had them there.

After dinner there was more playing, followed by story time with yours truly. I love reading, and I believe it is one of the most imperative activities you can do with a kid. I opened the large storybook to the chosen tale, made room for the kids around me on the couch, and began. I forget the details, but at one point the reading dissolved into me going on a temporary reading strike with the statement, "You guys can sit together, but I'm not reading if you are stepping on your brother." The book went on the floor, causing a minor meltdown. Senator observed silently;

---

[*]   I suspect he may have read Donald Trump's *The Art of the Deal.*

this was a new dimension to his world. Eventually bodies were repositioned, apologies were made, and the strike concluded peacefully to the satisfaction of all who were eager to know how the story ended.[*]

It was bedtime. The children hugged us, and we reminded them that we would see them the next month when they came north for Thanksgiving. Of course, there was an understood promise to watch *A Charlie Brown Thanksgiving* together. I was already looking forward to it. We said "good night" and the one-year old decided to give up her attempt to sample a little of the plant's dirt. Everyone was satisfied.

Heidi, Philip, Senator, and I continued the conversation over some pumpkin pie. Our evening had flown by. Senator and I were exhausted, and we weren't even sure why. As he said, we had basically just sat on the couch and watched the show. Maybe it was the fresh air, or maybe it was taking in the heaviness of the battlefields. Maybe it was because I was nursing watery eyes and a sniffly nose, due to either pollen outdoors or a recent mold infestation in my building at work. Of course, usually our trips consist of historical or nature-related activities, which tend to take place during the day. We're usually in for the night by 7:00pm. Perhaps our bodies were just not used to all this wild 'night life'.

*　　　　*　　　　*

Monday morning was chilly. Senator and I had a quiet breakfast together before checking out of our hotel. As he started the car, he put on a mix of music we had created the previous spring for our elopement. I was feeling

---

*　　most of all Senator

very satisfied with life, even though I knew we would be grounded from travel for at least six months due to work.

As we drove, we talked about the details involved in another upcoming house project. It seemed like all of our conversations involving our home took on the tone of the temporary. We continued to speak of changes and upgrades in terms of not just current benefit, but resale investment. I did not know if it was a temporary frame of mind or if we had made a permanent mental transition, but the trend continued.

Much like our mood, the ride home proved peaceful overall. In central Illinois we slowed to a crawl for about twenty minutes due to an accident, but most of the drive was smooth. The rest of our night was relaxed, too. As the credits for the 1942 sequel *The Invisible Agent* rolled, we each took a bite of pizza. It was not as good as the pizza Heidi had made us, but it was a sufficient start to our last date night of the long weekend. Work and chores would start again soon enough. *I wonder what that backflow valve will cost...*

Chapter 3
From Central Illinois
With Love:
Late May 2020

Note: All facts and figures in the following chapter are attributed to and verified within the Fort Pillow State Historic Park visitor center, battlefield site, and literature, as well as research from Nathan Bedford Forrest: In Search of the Enigma *by Eddy W. Davison and Daniel Foxx.*

Autumn rolled into the holidays, and we had the pleasure of celebrating them in Senator's mom's new home. We were all relieved that her old house had sold smoothly, and things were simpler, easier, and more enjoyable for her all around. The new place was smaller, too, meaning Senator and I would no longer be spending the night on major holidays. For the first time in fifteen years, we woke up in our own bed on Christmas morning. We had loved the years of slumber parties at her house, and now being home was its own special treat.

The new calendar year brought predictions about what a new decade in America would look like. (When such conversations arose, I sometimes stifled the urge to point out that technically a new decade would not start for another twelve months.) Regardless of what decade it was in, 2020 was definitely a presidential election year. Given the enormous amounts of money spent, and the leftists' hysterical reaction to the last presidential election, we assumed it would be wild. We had no idea just how crazy it would get.

January started off with a witch hunt impeachment based on hearsay. As it did not come close to meeting any convictable standards, and as the democrats did not hold the majority in the United States Senate, the president was cleared and kept his job. February and March ushered in the primary season, and Donald Trump easily nabbed the republican nomination in every state and territory that had voted. The democrats fought it out, gradually eliminating each of the almost twenty original contenders until it was down to Bernie Sanders and Joe Biden. Backed by big-money donors and well-heeled connections, Biden was coming out on top, though I believed the party would pull him at the last minute in favor of a stronger, hand-picked candidate. Then everyone forgot all about the primaries.

Since late January I had been loosely covering a story with my current events class about a flu-like virus birthed in the Wuhan province of China. My students were interested in it, offering questions and theories as to its origin and contagiousness. Most people I knew had never heard of it when we started talking about it, but interest and coverage was slowly building in February. By early

March daily updates appeared on the sidebars of news websites and as quick items on t.v. or radio reports. Then the second week of March came, and all other news was swallowed up.

Concerns over the Wuhan coronavirus (later renamed COVID-19 in response to claims that it was "racist" to name a disease after the region from which it came) shut down colleges and forced health care facilities and first responders to take extra precautions. We thought it was a sensible measure, and kept an eye on the situation. Then some places started canceling events. It seemed a little drastic, but the trend continued. We knew it would be a runaway train of changes when major professional sports started canceling games, and even their entire seasons. I could not imagine the money and domino effect of job loss that would entail. The media talked about the athletes; I thought about the men and women who attended the parking lots, ran light and sound systems, and sold hot dogs and beer.

The dirty snowball rolled downhill with lightning speed. Within one week, Senator had lost all of his mobile recording jobs, and I was working from home. It was a surreal blur. We were not fearful of the virus, but we followed the recommended health guidelines and diligently listened to all federal and state level press conferences to get primary source news from the doctors, scientists, and private-sector industries involved. As facts, data, and common sense converged, after about a month it became apparent that this was much more about control than illness. Infection and recovery rates were far more promising than we were originally told, yet many governors (mostly democrat) continued to pile on economic-killing, constitutionally-invalid, and inconsistent regulations. The population was supposed to stay at home to be safe, and houses of worship and small businesses were shuttered, but big box stores and strip clubs were just fine. You could not get necessary non-emergency surgery, but you could abort a baby. Many jobs were deemed "non-essential", but you were imperative if you sold marijuana or alcohol.

The government overreach mounted, with fascist-style enforcement that took cues directly from the socialist playbook. Citizens were encouraged to tattle on friends, family, and neighbors who violated orders. A salon owner was jailed for opening her legitimate business. Other small businesses were threatened with losing licenses unless they fully complied. Churches were harassed and vehicles were towed as they stood up for their 1st Amendment rights. It was shameful, and by May 1st many of us joined in a proverbial "Screw it!" and unquarantined ourselves, even attending protests to call out governors on their illegal orders.

The other side responded by doubling down, enacting more stringent measures, despite more accurate and very promising data concerning the virus. The less of a threat we realized it was, the harder they pressed down on the citizenry-- all in the name of "safety". The complicit media did their part by brainwashing people and working hard to create panic and divisions between those "following science" (doing whatever they were told regardless of data or reason), and those "denying science" (thinking for themselves, protecting their families and livelihoods, researching actual data, and keeping cool heads). Big government-types and those pushing toward globalism widely promoted the need for everyone to be vaccinated as soon as one could be developed-- never mind time to know if it was safe. They also spent millions (probably billions) of taxpayer dollars on contact tracers-- a modern army of minions to demand information about and compliance from anyone who tested positive for the virus and anyone with whom they had been in contact. As a result, gun, gun permit, and ammunition sales soared.

Does it sound like I'm writing a science fiction book, Reader? That is how it felt.[*] It soon became apparent that the population was falling into two distinct groups: those who believed in freedom and common sense with personal responsibility, and those who were driven by a rabid, illogical fear. You can guess which camp Senator and I fell into.

During all of this mess, I had become quite the expert at booking and canceling hotel reservations. When I first naively thought my school would only be shut down for two weeks, I took advantage of the written-off "act of God" days by booking a short trip to Fort Pillow, a Civil War site in Tennessee. That was quickly canceled, when virtually every museum and even outdoor park shut down. When the closures were extended over spring break, I had to move our planned Smoky Mountains National Park/ Fort Sumter/ Hampton Roads trip to June. It was irritating to postpone much-anticipated travel for another two-and-a-half months, so I decided to squeeze in a weekend at Fort

_____

[*]   Since then, someone clever renamed the mess 'Covid-1984' in
        reference to the Orwellian scenario.

Pillow over Memorial Day weekend, right between my spring and summer semesters of remote teaching. At least we would have something on the calendar to look forward to.

*   *   *

On the last Saturday in May, with just enough stuff for a three-day getaway, we left town. During the past two months, we had only left town for a dentist appointment, a few trips to a home improvement store, and to visit family.[*] All vacations are escapes, but this one felt like it more than usual. As we got on the highway, I was immediately pleased at the remembered feeling of freedom and anticipation that I always get on the first day of a trip. It was as though a little part of me was restored.

Sadly, Jingles, our G.P.S. companion during the past three years, had not yet been restored. She had recently developed the none-too-convenient characteristic of not accepting new addresses. This rendered her almost useless on trips. Thus, Senator had procured a different G.P.S. unit, which we unimaginatively dubbed Son of Jingles. *Just when she and I were finally getting along...*

The only thing on the agenda the first day was a few hundred miles of driving. Along with that, however, came an unofficial research project. The first thing we noted was the amount of traffic. It was a little lighter than one might expect on the Saturday before Memorial Day, but still far busier than one might expect from a state that was still supposed to be staying home except for absolutely necessary trips for essential goods and services. The stretch

---

[*] By comparison, we normally put an average of about 1800 miles on *each* of our cars per month!

between Springfield and St. Louis was especially hopping. That was encouraging. It was probably the only time in my life that I ever wished for heavy traffic.

Part two of our research consisted of noting the origin of the vehicles on the road. During our drive, we were on the soil of Illinois, Missouri, and Tennessee. Circumstantial logic would tell you that we should have encountered license plates from those three states. We did... as well as about twenty more. During our weekend, we saw represented locations from as far as Washington, California, New Mexico, Texas, Florida, New York, Connecticut, Minnesota, and others. This also made us smile heartily. "Look," I pointed out, upon seeing a large r.v.. "They must not have toilet paper or disinfectant in Wyoming!" Surely no one else was leaving their states for a vacation; they *must* all be on essential errands.

"Yep. It's too bad there are no grocery stores or doctors in Maryland," responded Senator as he indicated another out-of-state plate. Thank God there were still some Americans who valued freedom!

At home we had had a relatively cool spring, much to our delight. Now summer was upon us. It was already in the upper 80s, and well on its way to the high of 91°F. Any time we made a stop, we were glaringly aware that our bodies were not in hot weather mode yet. We were still in better shape than the numerous dead armadillos that littered the road about an hour south of St. Louis, though. Every few miles we saw another one, appearing both harmless and menacing at the same time. It sure looked like one of those spikes could pop a tire if a car wandered over them.

The first sign, we ignored. At least, I thought we did. When we passed the second sign advertising a confection known as fried pie, however, curiosity combined with our anti-quarantine rebellion got the better of us, and we exited the interstate. I believe our official excuse was that we needed gas. "We're in Tennessee..." Senator announced, as though suggesting that it was now somehow incumbent upon us to eat fried junk food. It might not have been the decision I would have made, but I was not arguing.

Just like the busy rest area we had visited in Missouri, no one was wearing masks. It was refreshingly normal-- like we were all reasonable human beings and not biohazards. I filled our tank. Senator filled our need to explore the local cuisine. It occurred to me that we had not had any non-homemade food in about ten weeks. I was not sure our stomachs wanted fried pie to be the debut, but here it was, nonetheless.

We slid into our seats and buckled up. I started the car and blasted the air conditioning. Senator carefully passed me the cherry crème pie he had chosen for me, while holding his maple nut pie. Though neatly folded over and sealed during the frying process, I still managed to send a blob of it right onto my jeans. At least it came out easily with bottled water and wet wipes. After a few bites of our own, and sampling each others' pies, we pronounced the fried pie rating as a solid C-. The texture of the crust was not unpleasant-- sort of like a soft calzone-- but the filling was more sugary than flavorful, and basically just gloppy. So now we know.

With our fried pie experiment concluded, we

continued deeper into Tennessee. "Well, that's something," I mused. A brown sign informed us that we had crossed through the birthplace of Isaac Hayes. It made us laugh to think of how far and different the soul music scene was from Nathan Bedford Forrest and the Tennessee Civil War cavalry we had come to study.

It was early evening when we arrived at our modest hotel. Inside a young and peppy girl with a very heavy Tenn-issipi* accent greeted us. There was a plexiglass barrier at the desk, but she was not wearing a mask. Neither were the two construction workers who were remodeling the lobby. Apparently the girl was new, so she was cautiously going through each step to check us in. When she ran into a minor question, her boss came to assist. He was wearing a mask, but he was very polite and did not seem to care that we were not wearing them. In fact, he graciously apologized that he was not yet allowed to serve the usual breakfast buffet, so he knocked a fair amount off of our bill.

Our room was on the humid side, but the air conditioner was strong, and everything was neat and clean. I think I might have wiped off the doorknobs and remote control with a disinfectant wipe, but maybe I didn't. I don't remember. I didn't really care. I felt truly relaxed... despite the toilet that required a semi-elaborate trick to flush.

We settled in and started to think about dinner that did not involve fried food or pie. At home I had looked up

---

* This is not any proper linguist term. It is only my description of one of the heavier-drawl and slower-speaking regions of the South. Typically I have heard it in western Tennessee and northern Mississippi, hence the elision.

a Mexican restaurant that did carryout. The idea appealed to Senator, so we plugged the address into Son of Jingles and headed out. Even without G.P.S., it should have been simple. Our hotel was just off the main highway, and the restaurant was on the main highway. I figured it should be south, but the address numbers went the wrong way. Son of Jingles took us in the correct direction as related to the numbers, but we ended up out of town near empty lots. It was then that the light bulb popped on, and I realized that it was one of those situations where the address numbers started from the middle of town and grew in opposite directions. Had the address included a "south" or "north", it would have helped. At any rate, we eventually found it.

I waited while Senator went in. Not only was no one wearing masks as they passed each other going through the door to the popular eatery, but customers filled the regularly-spaced tables inside. Back in Illinois, indoor dining was strictly verboten, and any maskless employee of a food establishment would probably be treated like a criminal. Again we relished both the normalcy and the peace God had given us, releasing us from any doubt several weeks before. It was freeing.

Back in the room we enjoyed our bountiful feast of hot Mexican food. It was delicious, far making up for the disappointment of fried pie. We watched a little news, but quickly shifted away from the many coronavirus-centered commercials. Instead, we were engrossed in a marathon of home remodeling shows. It was a marvelous distraction, and one that had us giddily imagining our potential future home. *As long as it doesn't have a toilet like the one in this bathroom*, I thought.

Senator had not been sleeping well the past few weeks. It was mostly due to a resurgence of his sleep apnea, but I suppose all of the fervent monitoring of daily-changing events was a contributing factor as well. Unfortunately, our first night away from home in months was not filled with quality sleep, either. It was far better than some nights we had recently experienced, but he definitely could have used a few more hours of shut-eye. Even so, when it came time to get ready for day's excursion, he was ready and eager to go.

As I mentioned, our hotel was not yet allowed to have their regular breakfast buffet, due to state rules regarding coronavirus. This was not an issue for me, since I am never hungry in the morning. Senator, however, usually has to eat, especially if it's going to be a long day. "I'll just grab something on the way," he said. It was an easy plan, so we headed north along the main highway.

In just a couple of miles, however, we had run out of "along the way". We turned off the main road and headed through rural land and into woods-- deep, thick, vine-canopied Tennessee woods. "This is it," I warned Senator. "There isn't anything else between here and where we are going."

He was not concerned. "That's okay. I'll make it until later." I felt bad for him, since later probably meant supper, and we had a hike planned. "After all," he added, "it's not like I'm hiking twenty miles with my knapsack on hard tack and salt pork." He had a point. We will always be amazed by the stamina of soldiers on both sides of the War

Between the States.[*]

As we toodled along the winding country road, we came to a fork. Perched on the triangular plot of land was an old and run-down white, wooden-sided building. It had probably needed updating since the 1950s. On it were painted the words "GROCERY" and "BAIT". *At least "GROCERY" comes first*, I thought. I was amazed to find any establishment in that region, so we pulled into the parking lot. "Maybe you can find a granola bar or muffin or something," I said. I figured there would be at least a small assortment of packaged snacks that one usually finds at a convenience store.

Senator agreed and went in. I waited in the car to see if Son of Jingles had sorted out his confusion as to our location. We were not lost-- it was a straightforward drive-- but the new G.P.S. was fairly certain Fort Pillow State Historic Park did not exist. We were determined to prove it wrong. As I fiddled with the thing, I glanced at my surroundings. A man was walking down the road, with the ultimate goal of stopping at the GROCERY BAIT for his morning can of pop. Another lady was waiting in a nearby vehicle as her partner ran in for some necessary item. Of most interest was the antique (but still apparently in daily use) rusty fish scale. It was a spring model, utilized by hanging a fish on the metal hook and seeing how far down the spring was pulled.

---

[*] There are many names for what is commonly known as the American Civil War: the War Between the States, the Second American Revolution, the Second War for Independence, the War of Northern Aggression, and others. Lately Senator's favorite has been that of Robert E. Lee: "the Recent Unpleasantness".

I started to wonder what was taking Senator so long, but I could see his form through the glass windows, so I assumed he had not been captured as a Yankee spy by descendants of Nathan Bedford Forrest's crew. Eventually he came out, grinning, with a square styrofoam carry-out container in his hand. "They made me breakfast!" he announced, proud of himself.

"Explain?..."

"Well, I saw they had a little deli counter, so I asked if they had any sort of breakfast sandwich. They didn't have anything like that, but the woman behind the counter said, 'We got sooome ee-eegggs. Waa-aant me to fix ya' soooommme?' So I said, 'Sure!' Then she asked if I wanted four, since they were 'smaa-aall'. I told her three were plenty. She asked how I wanted them, and if I wanted any meat or cheese. She even offered some toast." With that, he opened his container and dove into a lovely cheese omelet, garnished with a slice of heavily buttered white toast. For his princely and lovingly prepared meal, he had forfeited the sum of just $4.00. Well done.

We passed through a few more towns with populations smaller than an average family reunion, and finally we turned off to find the entrance to Fort Pillow State Historic Park. As the name suggested, the preserved Civil War fort site also doubled as a recreation area. As the road wound toward its terminus at the visitor center, we passed a camping area, a boat launch on a small lake, and an overlook of the Mississippi River. All were picturesque, but the best feature of the land was the snaking mounds of earthworks that remained from its use as a fortification more than a century-and-a-half ago. These can still be found on several battlefields in the South. In this case, they were constructed by Confederate soldiers.

The skies hinted at possible rain, so we wanted to take our hike to the partial fort reconstruction first. There were several trails in the park, so we ducked in the visitor center for a decent trail map before starting. Immediately we were greeted by an extremely friendly attendant at the desk. The 70-ish woman beamed. "Hah yeeww-all!" As we returned a smiling but more subdued greeting, she continued. "Where yeeww-all froo-oommm?" This was the normal question that visitor center employees and volunteers pose, and we had considered the matter carefully beforehand. Normally when out of state or country, we simply say "Chicago", and let the jokes flow as they may. Now, due to two months of bad national press surrounding inflated numbers of waning people catching coronavirus near the Windy City, we knew better than to associate ourselves with the supposed hottest Kung Flu[*] spot in the nation. We also knew we probably could not pull off a convincing southern Illinois accent, so we had decided on the relatively benign and safely vague answer of "Central Illinois". Neither location was exactly accurate, but they were roughly equal in their inaccuracy. Nevertheless, as she kept the polite conversation going, she slyly turned and slipped on a mask. We were the Illinois pariahs.

With map in hand, and already sweating in the heavy Tennessee humidity, we started the two-and-a-half mile round trip hike. It would be just the right length, especially since the lady at the visitor center had cautioned

---

[*]   another great nickname for the virus

us that the entire path was "moderate to strenuous". We crossed the short plank bridge and headed into the woods. Had it been about twenty degrees cooler and much drier, it would have been a perfect trek. The terrain took us through a comfortable variety of flat dirt, grassy meadow, gravel road, steep and rooted path, and eventually onto a grassy plateau. We had reached the reconstruction, which featured several cannon arranged in a large curve against a built-up wall. Beyond the wall was about a fifteen-foot ditch. Interestingly, the site of the fort used to be closer to the Mississippi River, but years of erosion had actually created more shoreline, effectively pushing the river further out. We could still see across it to Arkansas at one point, though.

It was muggy and buggy, so we did not stay at the top long. We just took a few pictures and started on the return trail. Along the way I watched for poison ivy, of which there was plenty. A few patches lining the sides of the trail sported the largest leaves I had ever seen on the plant. After seventeen years of coaching, Senator was finally starting to recognize it while hiking. A few times we also encountered other hikers, none of whom were masked. We have many times said that if we could stand Tennessee's climate, then its location, history, people, and politics would place it solidly on our list of places to move. Alas...

We were almost back to the parking lot, and I was panting hard. It was not from the strain; it was instead a combination of congestion and still being in my cool weather, thick-blooded mode.[*] We laughed, musing at how

_____

[*] I actually have no scientific basis for this, but lots of older people swear that their blood gets thinner when they age, and attribute their intolerance to cold to it. There may be something to it,

77

New Hampshire, known for its underestimated trail difficulty rating system, would have classified this "moderate to strenous" trail. "'Easy,'" Senator joked.

"'Wheelchair accessible',," I returned.

"'Good for children'...."

"'Stroller appropriate'...."

We also giggled about the spiked burrs we found littering the ground. "Look! A massive coronavirus outbreak!" we joked, referring to the ubiquitous enlarged photos of the virus that accompanied so many news reports. The heat and humidity were making us goofy. It was time for the air conditioning of the visitor center/ museum.

Fort Pillow, named for General Gideon Pillow[*], started out as a Confederate fort in 1861. The next year it was taken over by Union forces, and held until it was closed in 1864. That same year it was reopened, mainly for trade purposes. The real action then commenced. In April, General Nathan Bedford Forrest attacked the ill-prepared fort and demanded surrender. The terms would include taking all soldiers prisoner. If terms were refused, Forrest would proceed with full impact.

In fact, surrender was refused, and Forrest attacked mercilessly. During the melee, many Union men were

---

however, as bodies do adapt. A northern Canadian will be sweating at 60°F, while a tropical dweller will be piling on the heavy clothes at the same temperature. Those of us who live in the middle are just never comfortable.

[*] If you ask me, this is perhaps the worst person one could have chosen to name a fort after, as Pillow's main role two years before at Fort Donelson was to abandon it *and* his men to the attack by General Ulysses S. Grant.

78

killed, and of those a disproportionately high number were black soldiers. While original reports claimed that Forrest ordered this slaughter, further clarification revealed that some of his men did this on their own, and he repeatedly gave orders to stop, even shooting one of his own men for disobeying. There were also horrific rumors of men being buried alive in the aftermath.

Ultimately, the entire incident was thrown to a Congressional hearing. Interestingly, many testimonies from Federal officers (including that of Forrest's main nemesis, General William T. Sherman) absolved Forrest of many of the crimes of which he was accused. One report suggested that he actually prevented scores more deaths of Union soldiers. Most historians also believe that gruesome tales of pre-death burials were grossly overestimated. If they had taken place at all, facts pointed to such occurrences on the Union side, and due to confusion more than anything. Any any rate, the papers had a field day, and the battle was evermore referred to as the Fort Pillow Massacre.

Due to the nature of the event, we had done significant research on the details and the 'Wizard of the Saddle' himself. The museum's artifacts seemed to support a balanced and fair analysis of the facts of the situation, while mourning and respecting those who were wrongly executed in the act of surrender. On protected display was an original copy of the Congressional findings. I would have loved to dig into that book.

We meandered through the rest of the small museum, watching the summary film in the cool, dark theatre and viewing more artifacts of daily soldier life. One exhibit featured a replica supply wagon with everything from homemade lye soap to an enlisted man's prayer book. Another display explained the important role of the Mountain Howitzer gun. This cannon easily broke down for animal transport over rough or uneven terrain. Upon arrival, it could be conveniently reassembled for the job at hand.

We must be making progress in our addictions; we bypassed a Nathan Bedford Forrest biography in the gift shop. It was tempting, but we already had two great resources on him, and there was probably nothing else this one would have added. We have been trying to keep our library concise and meaningful. "Wow, that was a very mature decision for us," I pronounced.

"Yeah, especially with no adult supervision around," Senator pointed out.

One flier listed a historian talk about the various flags the Confederacy used, but there was no sign of the event taking place. I think it must have been scheduled and then canceled when things were up in the air regarding reopening. We did not mind; we were hot and hungry, and we already knew about several iterations of the flag. It was only mid-afternoon, but there were no other places we wanted to visit in the area. The only other Tennessee site on our list was several hours away, so it would have to wait for another trip.

We left Fort Pillow, satisfied with our research and our hike. I was quite hungry by this time, so we grabbed a sandwich near our hotel. The mercury had reached the low 90s, and we were craving cool showers. Cleaning up felt wonderful, and though we could be accused of being lazy, lying around binge-watching more home improvement shows with no references to pandemics felt wonderful, too. Thankfully they had been recorded before humans stopped interacting normally.

Our forced relaxation culminated with a pizza with dripping garlic sauce later that night. (No one was accusing us of a healthy weekend.) We also indulged in more quiet time together. "I hope you don't feel like it was a waste to drive down here for a half-day excursion," I said, a little apologetically.

"Not at all," answered Senator without hesitation. "I really think we needed it. I'm having fun."

"Me too!" I was glad he felt that way. We must have been doing something right, because we both slept better than we had in a long time.

*   *   *

Monday was Memorial Day. We did not usually travel Memorial Day weekend, but we were not missing anything at home. This year our local V.F.W. hall had canceled its service due to the governor's illegally extended quarantine orders. I expect many of the senior citizens might have stayed home anyway, but it should have been their choice-- not some power-hungry bureaucrat's decision. We put on our matching shirts that honored veterans and began our day.[*]

There was no breakfast at the hotel, but this time we went a different direction, so we found a quick bite to take on the road. The traffic was clipping along well, and it was particularly busy around St. Louis. Again we were pleased to see vehicles from so many different states on the road. It

---

[*] See Appendix B

had been a long way to come for just one destination, but the freedom of driving a considerable distance had taken on new meaning. We were renewed, even when we had to stop for twenty minutes in central Illinois for an accident.

At home we could see a few more cars than usual on our short, dead-end street. "Looks like the neighbors are having a party," said Senator. *Good. I hope people are congregating and hugging their loved ones and sharing food and having a gay ol' time*, I thought as we unpacked the car. If our nanny state would try to keep us separate and at home, we would find ways around it ourselves.

We finished putting a few items away, and I separated some laundry. When I thought of something I wanted to check on the wall calendar, I went over to flip up a page or two. To my surprise, it was not just information that spilled out; a few ants scattered around from somewhere between August and September. A quick scan revealed, of course, that there were more in the vicinity. As I grudgingly set up the bait traps, I had a firm suspicion that Governor Pritzker had dispatched the pests, in retaliation for our sneaky weekend away.

Afterword

123, 123, 133, 165, 107, 187, 285, 363, and... 87. *Sigh*. Those are the progressive page counts of my books in this series. Never, while planning more Civil War excursions, another jaunt to Ontario, and a magnificent return to the land of our elopement, did I imagine that our travel plans would come to a screeching halt. If I had imagined such an interruption to what has become one of the natural components of our relationship, I likely would have attributed it to an unfortunate event due to illness or economics-- not a global plan-demic. Yet, there you have it. We were still able to enjoy an easy, peaceful trip as official 'newlyweds' and exploring another two battlefields before the hammer dropped. Then being told by a power-hungry governor for no true reason to stay home like naughty grounded children made it absolutely necessary to get away one more time.

That covered the first year. "What about the second year?" you may be wondering, since each book in this series covers two years. The short answer is, we did not travel at all from June 2020 through the publication date. In fact, we set a record for the most consecutive nights in our own bed since we have been together. The reasons are too vast to expound upon, but I may do so at another time in another type of book.

Basically, there were four main deterrents. First of all, most indoor and even many outdoor sites remained closed, driven by fear of contagion or lawsuits. Secondly, though it soon became apparent that the virus was not nearly as bad as originally hyped, many places were now jumping on the virtue-signaling bandwagon of requiring absolutely useless masks. To my knowledge, I am not a surgeon, a bank robber, or a Muslim, so I refused to pay to be part of that fraud. There was also the fact that we had blown the vacation fund on a much-needed shower remodel. (Well, that and more ammo.) Finally and most compelling, a week after we returned from Tennessee, riots and uncontrolled violence, cheered on by democrat leaders, broke out around the country, making us want to stick closer to home for awhile.

Thus, year number two was a bust. Thus, you can brag that you read an entire book in just a few hours. Thus, hopefully you paid less for this one than the others. Once 'the lights go on again all over the world' I fully intend to make it up to you (and me).

~Wendy V
May 2021

Appendix A:
Cabin Editing Candidates

The following items, in alphabetical order, were on the initial ballot as potentials for elimination. (Non-winners may still be in the running for future removal.):

1965ish Cushions-- plenty of better options; we've managed without them this long

1972ish Flowers-- bad color scheme; too dusty; overshadowed by beauty of real wildflowers on property

8-Track Player-- hasn't been used since Trudeau Sr.'s administration; two-thirds of family probably could not even identify it

Cooking Utensils with Decorative Glossy Vegetables on Ends-- unusable; plenty of real cooking utensils

Easy Stripper-- no, just kidding; this could actually be a useful product for removing old paint, but I couldn't resist incorporating the name

Flat Basket-- no one uses; no one can think of what they would use it for

Leopard-Print Cloth-- surely someone, somewhere must need this more than anyone at the cabin

Mystery Pants-- enough said

Old Farm People Figurines-- too breakable; more Kansas than Ontario

Pilgrim Silhouettes (1ˢᵗ Set)-- more colonial than north woods; doubles

Pilgrim Silhouettes (2ⁿᵈ Set)-- see above

Reader's Digest Condensed Books (Multiple Volumes)-- no one reads; takes up too much shelf space from books people do read

Sailor Lamp-- not bad, but why have it if no one ever uses it?

Appendix B:
Veteran Shirt

I found these shirts on a patriotic website a few years ago. They are black, with the official P.O.W./M.I.A. logo of a man's profile in a prison camp with a guard in a tower in the background. The front contains the motto "You are not forgotten". The back has the following poem:

> It is the soldier, not the reporter,
> > who has given us freedom of the press.
>
> It is the soldier, not the poet,
> > who has given us freedom of speech.
>
> It is the soldier, not the campus organizer,
> > who has given us the freedom to demonstrate.
>
> It is the soldier, not the lawyer,
> > who has given us the right to a fair trial.
>
> It is the soldier who salutes the flag,
> > and whose coffin is draped by the flag,
> > who allows the protester to burn the flag.